Heroes of the Scots-Irish in America

by
BILLY KENNEDY

AMBASSADOR
Belfast Northern Ireland **Greenville** South Carolina

Heroes of the Scots-Irish in America
© 2000 Billy Kennedy
ISBN 1 84030 085 X
First published September, 2000

THE SCOTS-IRISH CHRONICLES

The Scots-Irish in the Hills of Tennessee (published 1995)
The Scots-Irish in the Shenandoah Valley (published 1996)
The Scots-Irish in the Carolinas (published 1997)
The Scots-Irish in Pennsylvania and Kentucky (published 1998)
Faith and Freedom - The Scots-Irish in America (published 1999)
Heroes of the Scots-Irish in America (published 2000)

PRINTED IN NORTHERN IRELAND

Published by

Causeway Press

Ambassador Productions Ltd.,
Providence House
Ardenlee Street,
Belfast, BT6 8QJ
www.ambassador-productions.com

Emerald House Group Inc.
427 Wade Hampton Boulevard,
Greenville,
South Carolina 29609
www.emeraldhouse.com

About *the Author*

THIS SIXTH BOOK by Northern Ireland journalist and author Billy Kennedy is the latest in the popular series of Scots-Irish Chronicles which tell the absorbing story of the 18th century settlements on the American frontier by immigrants from the Irish province of Ulster. Previous books in the series, published and circulated widely in the United Kingdom and the United States, were The Scots-Irish in the Hills of Tennessee (published 1995), The Scots-Irish in the Shenandoah Valley (1996), The Scots-Irish in the Carolinas (1997), The Scots-Irish in Pennsylvania-Kentucky (1998) and Faith and Freedom: The Scots-Irish in America (1999). Billy Kennedy, who lives in Co Armagh, has been a leading Northern Ireland journalist for the past 30 years, occupying the roles of news editor, assistant editor and leader writer with the Belfast News Letter, the main morning newspaper in Northern Ireland, during a career which spanned 1974-1998. He is now a freelance journalist, author and public relations consultant, combining news, feature and sports coverage in Northern Ireland for national press and media outlets in the United Kingdom and the Irish Republic. On his regular visits to the United States, he lectures on the subject of the Scots-Irish at universities, colleges, historical and genealogical societies and public authorities in cities and towns of the south eastern American states. He is married with a grown-up daughter.

How sleep the Brave who sink to rest,
All their country's honors blest!

•••

Dedication

This book is dedicated to my loving wife Sally,
daughter Julie and my parents.

•••

"The Lord gave the Word. Great was the company of those
that published it." PSALM 68, verse 11.

•••

The author acknowledges the help and support given to him in the
compilation of this book by Dr. Samuel Lowry, of Ambassador
Productions/Causeway Press, Northern Ireland and Tomm Knutson, of
Emerald House, Greenville, South Carolina.

•••

Cover pictures: *Fall of The Alamo by Robert Jenkins Onderdonk, used*
by kind permission of Friends of the Governor's Mansion, Austin,
Texas. Inset illustrations - Andrew Jackson, Ulysses S. Grant and
Thomas Jonathan "Stonewall" Jackson. Andrew Jackson - Oil on
Canvas. Artist: Ralph E. W. Earl. Date: c1833. Courtesy of The
Hermitage Home of Andrew Jackson, Nashville, Tennessee.

List *of contents*

Foreword *from the United States*

Dr. John Rice Irwin

his is the sixth book which the Northern Irelander Billy Kennedy has written about the remarkable and often little noted influences the Scots-Irish people have had on the history, development, growth and shape of the United States of America. I've had the pleasure of penning the foreword to each of these books and here I come back to "say a few words" with respect to this, the latest publication on the subject.

The previous volumes have dealt with the settlements and undoubted influences of the Scots-Irish in various political regions of the United States: the Hills of Tennessee, the Shenandoah Valley, the Carolinas, Pennsylvania and Kentucky, as well as chronicling the achievements of these people in protecting their Faith and Freedom.

As the title Heroes of the Scots-Irish infers, this book deals more with the personal lives of individual people of Scots-Irish ancestry. And perhaps this is the most meaningful method of understanding a community, a state or a nation.

What better way is there to know the history of a people, than to understand the personal and family lives of those individuals comprising the lobby? The history of a society, an ethnic group, or a political unit is often told in general overall terms; examining the form of government, the military engagements, the acts of the legislature, the various political parties and such.

How can one not be excited and inspired by reading the truly fabulous life of soldier, statesmen and US President Andrew Jackson or to follow Davy Crockett from his log cabin home at Greene county in East Tennessee to the Halls of Congress and to his heroic death at The Alamo? Nine of those who died at The Alamo were born in Ireland, and several dozen of the other "Texian" victims were of Scots-Irish roots.

The lives of such colorful and influential men as Thomas Jonathan "Stonewall" Jackson, JEB Stuart, Sam Houston, Kit Carson, Woodrow Wilson, James Robertson and John Donelson and scores of other Scots-Irish heroes which appear in this volume are as fascinating and so eventful, so romantic and so adventurous as to excite the soul and to cause one to develop a thirst to know more about them.

And therein lies the importance of this book - to titillate the reader to journey farther into the legendary lives of these individuals and to enjoy, profit and be guided and inspired by their lives

If this book and these tremendous real-life, human-interest stories accomplishes this, Billy Kennedy will have reached his goal, and a valuable contribution to the history and understanding of our people will have been completed.

DR JOHN RICE IRWIN,
Director of Museum of Appalachia, Norris, Tennessee

• **DR JOHN RICE IRWIN** is founder and director of the Museum of Appalachia at Norris, Tennessee, 15 miles from the city of Knoxville. The extensive East Tennessee farm village has gained national and international recognition for its concentration on the rich culture and folklore of the Appalachian mountain region. Dr Irwin has been a teacher, farmer, businessman, historian, author and his wide range of interests also extends to the music of his south eastern home region. His family is of Scots-Irish and Welsh extraction.

Billy Kennedy presents a copy of The Scots-Irish in Pennsylvania and Kentucky to bluegrass singer Ricky Skaggs. They are joined by John Rice Irwin and his wife Elizabeth.

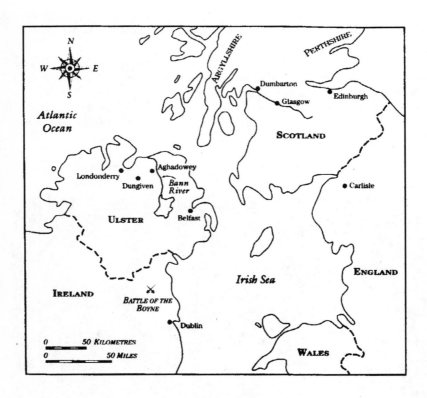

England, Scotland and Ireland.

Foreword *from Northern Ireland*

Cllr. Dr. Ian Adamson OBE, MLA

illy Kennedy continues his Scots-Irish Chronicles with his enthralling insight into the lives of their greatest heroes. In the further celebration of the rich historical heritage of America, due acknowledgement is given to the pioneering efforts of these Ulster Presbyterian settlers.

In America's Historylands we read: "Of Scotch-Irish stock was James Robertson, who founded a settlement (the site of present Elizabethton, Tennessee!) on the banks of the Watauga River. For mutual protection against Indians and outlaws, the Wataugans in 1772 formed the first independent government established by white men west of the Appalachians. During the Revolution they placed themselves under the mantle of North Carolina, but had to beat off attack by England's Indian's allies. In 1779, Robertson recruited a party and led them down the frozen Cumberland River. On snow-covered bluffs they founded Nashboro (Nashville). After the War, the Wataugans' Scotch-Irish blood boiled because North Carolina continued to ignore their needs, indeed referred to the settlers as 'off-scourings of the earth'. In 1784, the Wataugans resolved to break away 'forming themselves into a separate government'." [1]

The resulting State of Franklin kept its independence for four years before finally succumbing because of economic hardship. However, this one example of Scots-Irish settlement highlights the tenaciousness of purpose and the independence of attitude which these settlers brought to their new country of domicile.

The extent of Scots-Irish settlement is well illustrated in this listing by Ulster folklorist and historian the Rev W. F. Marshall: "Ulster's mark on America is also visible in its place names. There are eighteen towns in the United States named after Belfast. There are seven Derrys, nine Antrims and sixteen Tyrones. There is a Coleraine in Massachusetts. New Hampshire has Stewartstown. Hillsborough is in Washington, Illinois, North Dakota and Wisconsin. Maine has Newry. Ohio has Banbridge. In twelve states there are twelve Milfords." [2]

While their ability to triumph over adversity speaks highly of the strength of character of the Scots-Irish settlers, this uncompromising determination to establish themselves in their new land had a darker side to it - their ever advancing settlements contributed greatly to the destruction of the Indian nation.

The Indians, as historian Fred A. Shannon explained, were "a settled people living in villages and practising an advanced stage of agricultural economy."

"They had many hundreds of cleared acres of land on which they grew corn, sometimes a hundred bushels to an acre, in addition to an equal amount of such vegetables as pumpkins, squashes and beans. For lack of any indigenous animals that could be domesticated for draft purposes, hand implements were the only recourse for cultivation, but for several generations the white man (who looked upon them as savages because of their different complexions and habits!) failed to excel these Indians in the quality of produce or the size of crops to the acre." [3]

Throughout all the various Indian uprisings that punctuated the early history of America, the central thread was to be the Indians' attempt to put a stop to the continuing white encroachments upon their lands.

The Indians fought bravely, their most prominent victory being at the Battle of Greasy Grass (Little Big Horn) River when Chief Sitting Bull's braves wiped out General George Armstrong Custer's cavalry detachment in 1876, but more unusually they suffered continuing defeats, including the infamous and needless massacre of nearly 250 Indian men, women and children at Wounded Knee Creek in South Dakota on December 29, 1890.

The American expansion westward was pioneered by Ulster-Scots such as Tennessean Davy Crockett. Virginia-born Sam Houston, also of Ulster descent, organised the rebellion of the Scots-Irish settlers and others in Texas against the Mexicans and established the Republic of Texas. The famous Battle of The Alamo, fought in March, 1836, was viewed by the Texans as a heroic effort in their struggle for independence.

Not unnaturally, President Antonio de Santa Anna of Mexico took a very different view and considered them traitors. The Texas Revolution of 1835-36 resulted from several grievances against Mexico, the most important being the subversion by Santa Anna of the 1824 Constitution and his assumption of dictatorial powers.

The Texans won the first battle at San Antonio (the Battle of Bexar!), with the defeat of General Martin Perfecto de Cos on December 10, 1835, but Mexican forces numbering more than 6,000 appeared at San Antonio on February 23, 1836 and besieged The Alamo, a fortress near the town.

The Alamo was defended by a force of 189 Texans, led by William Barrett Travis and, including Davy Crockett and Jim Bowie, another Tennessean. On March 6, the Mexicans made an overwhelming assault against the post and, on capturing it, killed off the defenders. However, on March 15, Texas had declared her independence and Santa Anna's forces were defeated by the main Texas army under General Sam Houston in April.

An intriguing narrative of The Alamo, written by the fine Mexican soldier Vicente Filisola, who was present among the Mexican assailants on March 6, 1836, shows what many Mexicans felt about Santa Anna's judgment at the time.

"Considering the disposition he made for attack, our loss should have been still greater if all the cannon in the fort could have been placed on the walls, but the houses inside prevented it, and, from their situation, they could only fire in front. Furthermore, they had not a sufficient number of gunners. Indeed, artillery cannot be improvised as readily as rebellions. Also our movement from the right and the left upon the north front, and the movement executed by Minon and Morales with their column on the western salient, changing the direction from the southern front as instructed, rendered unavailable the pieces of artillery which the enemy had established on the other three fronts.

"Finally, the place remained in the power of the Mexicans and all the defenders were killed. It is a source of deep regret, that after the excitement of the combat, many acts of atrocity were allowed which are unworthy of the gallantry and resolution with which this operation had been executed, and stamp it with an indelible stain in the annals of history.

"These acts were reproved at the time by those who had the sorrow to witness and, subsequently, by the whole army, who certainly were not habitually animated by such feelings, and who heard with disgust and horror, as becomes brave and generous Mexicans who feel none but noble and lofty sentiments, of certain factors which forebear to mention and wish for the honour of the Mexican Republic had never taken place.

"In our opinion, the blood of the soldiers as well as that of the enemy was shed in vain, for the mere gratification of the inconsiderate, puerile and guilty vanity of reconquering Bexar by force of arms, and through a bloody conquest. As we have said, the defenders of The Alamo were disposed to surrender, upon the sole condition that their lives be spared.

"Let us even grant that they were not so disposed - what could the wretches do, being surrounded by 5,000 men, without proper means of resistance, no possibility of retreating, nor any hope of receiving proper and sufficient reinforcements to compel the Mexicans to raise the siege?

"Had they been supplied with all the resources needed that weak exposure could not have withstood for one hour the fire of our twenty pieces of artillery, which, if properly directed, would have crushed it to atoms and levelled down the inner buildings. The massacre of The Alamo, of Goliad, of Refugio, convinced the rebels that no peaceable settlement could be expected and that they must conquer, or die, or abandon the fruits of ten years of sweat and labour, together with their fondest hopes from the future." [4]

The following United States Presidents have been of direct Ulster descent: Andrew Jackson (1829-37), James Knox Polk (1845-49), James Buchanan (1857-61), Andrew Johnson (1865-69), Ulysses S. Grant (1869-77), Chester Alan Arthur (1881-85), Grover Cleveland (1885-89 and 1893-97), Benjamin Harrison (1889-93), William McKinley (1897-1901), Woodrow Wilson (1913-21), Richard Millhouse Nixon (1969-74), Jimmy Carter (1977-81) and Bill Clinton (1993-2000). Presidents Theodore Roosevelt, Harry Truman and George Bush are also reputed to have family links to the north of Ireland.

Many other famous Americans have some Ulster ancestry, from writers such as Stephen Foster, Edgar Allan Poe and Mark Twain to inventor Cyrus McCormick, actor James Stewart and astronauts Neil Armstrong, Edward H. White and James B. Irwin.

John Hughes, the first Roman Catholic archbishop of New York was born at Augher, Co Tyrone, and emigrated to America in 1817, during a second great exodus from Ireland which occurred a century after the Presbyterian immigrations from Ulster. This second wave was mainly composed of Irish Roman Catholics fleeing from a land devastated by the Great Famine. Hughes's successor and first American cardinal John McCloskey, was born in Dungiven, Co Londonderry.

There are many modern Americans who still take pride in their descent from Ulster-Irish families. Billy Kennedy's highly popular Scots-Irish Chronicles, now extended over six publications, is no exception. Defiant and aggressive, the Scots-Irish Presbyterians were the first pioneers on the American frontier. In fighting for freedom and equality, they became the fathers and mothers of democracy in the United States and left their mark on the history of the nation.

Councillor Dr IAN ADAMSON, OBE, MLA,
*Member of the Northern Ireland Assembly for
the constituency of East Belfast.
Former Lord Mayor of Belfast.
Author of various historical books on Ulster.*

1, America's Historylands, National Geographic Society, Washington DC (1962).
2, W. F. Marshall, Ulster Sails West, Genealogical Publishings Co Inc. Baltimore (1979)
3, Fred A. Shannon, American Farmers' Movements, Anvil Press, Princeton, New Jersey (1957)
4, Filisola, Vicente, in Moquin (ed.) A Documentary History of the Mexican Americans (1971).

• Books by Dr Ian Adamson: The Cruthin (1974), Bangor - Light of the World (1979), The Battle of Moira (1980), The Identity of Ulster (1982), The Ulster People (1991), 1690 - William and the Boyne (1995), Dalaradia - Kingdom of the Cruthin (1998).

Hi! Uncle Sam
Virginia sent her brave men,
The North paraded grave men,
That they might not be slave men,
But ponder this with calm:
The first to face the Tory,
And the first to lift Old Glory
Made your war an Ulster story:
Think it over, Uncle Sam!

Hi! Uncle Sam!
Wherever there was fighting,
Or wrong that needed righting,
An Ulsterman was sighting
His Kentucky gun with care:
All the road to Yorktown,
From Lexington to Yorktown,
From Valley Forge to Yorktown,
That Ulsterman was there!

W. F. MARSHALL (REV), CO. TYRONE

1

Andrew Jackson, *hero of New Orleans and American President, and his adoring wife, Rachel*

Andrew Jackson, the son of Co Antrim-born parents, more than anyone else, prepared the way for the enormous expansion of the American nation during the first four decades of the 19th century and his pivotal role in the War of 1812 ensured that the expansive territories on the south-western frontier did not fall back into British and Spanish hands.

Jackson's great triumphs as a soldier climaxed at the Battle of New Orleans and, of this encounter, he observed with considerable satisfaction: "The morning of January 8, 1815 will be recollected by the British nation, and always hailed by every true American."

In the American mind, the victory over the British at New Orleans was all down to Andrew Jackson's sterling leadership and he remained a popular hero across the nation for the rest of his life. Old Hickory - Hero of New Orleans - had restored the confidence of the nation and he provided reassurance in its ability to maintain its freedom and independence against heavy odds.

From his days growing up as a youth in the Waxhaws region of the Carolinas during the Revolutionary War period, Andrew Jackson developed a loathing for British colonial interests on American soil. His two brothers Hugh and Robert were casualties during the War and his widowed mother Elizabeth, a woman of extraordinary courage and determination, died from cholera fever in 1780 while attending sick nephews on a British prison ship in Charleston harbour.

Andrew, who as a 12-year-old received a facial wound from the sabre of a British soldier during an affray in the Waxhaws, was embittered by these deaths and, alone in the world at the age of 14, he vowed his revenge. More than 30 years later, just before the Battle of New Orleans, he told his wife Rachel that "retaliation and vengeance" characterised his attitude to the British and their Spanish and Creek Indian allies.

His personal experiences during the Revolutionary War shaped Andrew Jackson's character and purpose in life. He emerged with deep patriotic and nationalistic convictions, perceiving himself to be in a struggle for the liberties of his people and not forgetting the price that others had paid to secure them.

"I owe to the British a debt of retaliatory vengeance. Should our forces meet, I trust I shall pay the debt - she is in conjunction with Spain arming the hostile Indians to butcher our women and children," said Jackson, whose parents Andrew and Elizabeth had left their home at Boneybefore near Carrickfergus in Ulster in 1765 for Charleston in South Carolina, sailing from the Co. Antrim port of Larne.

The Jackson family were of Scottish lowland Presbyterian stock who had been in the north of Ireland from the mid-17th century and Andrew was born at the Waxhaws on March 15, 1767, a few weeks after the death of his father.

Andrew Jackson's youthful years were spent in the rough, tough world of the late 18th century Carolina frontier and this prepared him for the rigours of life as a soldier, lawyer, politician and statesman. He moved from being an apprentice saddler to become a teacher, at the age of 17, and eventually a lawyer at 20. He practiced law in Monroe, Anson county, and was public prosecutor of North Carolina's western district.

Jackson moved to the Tennessee country with others in 1788, trekking along the Wilderness Road over the Allegheny Mountains and arriving in Nashville, which was starting to expand out from its original Fort Nashborough log cabined frontier station. He opened a law office and met his wife Rachel Donelson, daughter of the settlement founder Colonel John Donelson, while staying as a boarding guest in her widowed mother's home.

Rachel had been married before, to Kentuckian Lewis Robards, who started divorce proceedings but dropped these without telling his estranged wife. This meant that Rachel unwittingly committed bigamy when she married Andrew in 1791, but when Robards later was granted a divorce, the couple remarried and, although they had no children, they had a very happy 27-year marriage. Rachel, and even Andrew, had to endure much slander and insults over the impropriety of their marriage and it became an issue during election times.

Jackson even fought a duel in Kentucky in 1806 with a Charles Dickinson, who spoke harshly of Rachel. Dickinson died from bullet wounds in the pistol shoot-out, while Jackson had rib and chest wounds, but survived. Duels were commonplace on the American frontier at the time, but the Dickinson incident was an unfortunate chapter in Jackson's life, and it took him several years to live it down.

Rachel, even though she was of a family of ten, inherited a substantial amount of property and money from her father's estate and Andrew, until then not a man of great means, benefited and his influence in Nashville expanded considerably.

By 1804, the couple were living at The Hermitage, outside Nashville, then a plantation log house and farm, and by 1819 this homestead had made way for a luxury brick house and expansive estate. Jackson's political career began in the Constitutional Convention of Tennessee in the mid-1790s and he was the first Congressman for the state, and later elected a US senator. In between, however, his military prowess came to the fore and this established himself as a household name across America.

Jackson was appointed major general of the Tennessee militia in 1802 and for the next 20 years he was seen as essentially a military man. His first major assignment in the regular army came in 1812 when the war department in Washington ordered his Tennessee soldiers to Natchez and there dismissed them. Jackson refused to obey orders and he marched his men back to Tennessee, earning for himself in that episode the title of 'Old Hickory'. A year on, he engaged his men against the Creek Indians at Talladega, and went on to triumph in other battles against the tribes. The Treaty of Fort Jackson, concluded in 1814, led to the transfer of most of the Creek lands in Alabama and southern Georgia to white settlers.

In May, 1814, Jackson was ordered to defend the Gulf coast against an expected British invasion and, after leading his troops into Florida and seizing the key port of Pensacola, marched to New Orleans, where, on the morning of January 8, 1815, he routed the British in a battle that has become immortalised in the annals of American history.

Jackson's army consisted of Tennesseans, Kentuckians, Blacks, Indians and Creoles and, when heavy British artillery fire failed to dislodge them from their location at the dried-up Rodriguez River, British commander Edward Pakenham ordered 6,500 Crown soldiers to attack head-on. Within 30 minutes 2,000 British soldiers were killed or wounded, while only 13 American fatalities were reported.

Theodore Roosevelt, in his book Naval War of 1812, said the American soldiers deserved great credit for doing so well. He added: "Greater credit still belongs to Andrew Jackson, who, with his cool head and quick eye, his stout heart and and strong hand, stands out in history as the ablest general the United States has produced from the outbreak of the Revolution down to the beginning of the Great Rebellion".

While Jackson may have had his critics over the manner of his victory at New Orleans through the imposition of martial law, suspension of habeas corpus and the execution of mutinous militiamen, he won acclaim throughout the nation and, to many, he was second only to General George Washington in service to the fledgling American republic. Interestingly, Jackson earned 5,000 dollars a year plus expenses as US army general, the same salary he received as governor of Florida.

Over the next few years Jackson successfully negotiated land treaties in Georgia, Alabama, Mississippi, Tennessee, and Kentucky with the Cherokee, Choctaw and Chickasaw Indian tribes. In 1818, he led troops back into Florida, this time to suppress the Seminole Indians, and again seized Pensacola and caused an international crisis by ordering the execution of two British subjects suspected of arming the Seminole tribes.

Jackson's hardline stance was vindicated in 1819 when he supervised the transfer of Florida from the Spanish to the United States and later he served as territorial governor there for three months during the establishment of state government. His remit extended to captain-general of Cuba, which meant complete military command throughout the highly volatile region.

Jackson resigned his Army commission on June 1, 1821 and in November of that year he and Rachel left Florida for their Hermitage home in Tennessee, where he set about resuming his political career with a vigour which eventually led him to the White House in 1828 for the start of two Presidential terms.

His war service and spell in the swamp heat of Florida took serious toll of Jackson's health. He had two bullets lodged in his body, one of which regularly formed abscesses and produced coughing spasms which led to massive haemorrhages. He also contracted dysentery and malaria and developed bronchitis which was to plague him for the rest of his life.

Despite his health strictures, however, Jackson managed to soldier on and for the next two decades as a national politician and statesmen he articulated the doctrine of Jacksonian Democracy, being effectively founder of the Democratic Party. This argued that it was the obligation of the United States government to grant no privilege that aides one class over another, to act as honest broker between classes, and to protect the weak and defenceless against the abuses of the rich and powerful.

It was said Andrew Jackson looked beyond the overarching institutions of American life, linked as they were to inherited wealth. To the dismay of Virginia and New England dynasties that had held the Presidency since the country's founding, Jackson was the first President whose name meant only what he himself could make it mean.

He challenged the power of Eastern banks, making credit available to the West, and resisted threats of secession from the South. By promoting the west and by holding America together, Jackson set a course for the common man within the nation. After his Presidency, candidates running for office searched in their backgrounds not for degrees from the university of Virginia or Harvard, but for a log cabin to incorporate in their campaign manifesto.

Tragically, Rachel Jackson died a few weeks after Andrew was elected for his first four-year term as President. After just recovering from the shock of the death their adopted 16-year-old Indian son Lyncoya, she was devastated by the public accusations during the Presidential campaign of "adultery and bigamy" resulting from her marriage to Jackson before a divorce from her first husband Lewis Robards was sanctioned. Heartbroken that she was targeted in this way, Rachel's physical and mental condition rapidly declined and although Andrew tried frantically to rally her, she died on December 22, 1828 and was buried in the garden of The Hermitage on Christmas Eve. One of the pall-bearers at the funeral was Sam Houston, then Governor of Tennessee and a close aide of Andrew Jackson.

For several days, the new President was inconsolable and he told his aides: "a loss so great can be compensated by no earthly gift". He had to prepare for the trip to Washington to begin his Presidency, but until the day he died in 1845 Andrew grieved for a wife who was so dear to him.

For most of his life, Andrew Jackson had never been a particularly religious man, but things changed for him on Sunday July 15, 1838 when he joined the Presbyterian Church. Both his mother and wife were both devoted Church members until their deaths and he had promised Rachel he would join, but had postponed a decision because he felt that as a politician a public display of his religion might be regarded as "hypocritical".

Now retired, Jackson consulted the Rev James Smith who ministered at The Hermitage Church, which he had built for Rachel in 1823, and admitted he felt more identified with the Presbyterian Church than with any other denomination.

During the July 15, 1836 service, Jackson rose in his pew to announce that he wanted to join the Church, and further declared his belief in its doctrines, and resolved to obey the Presbyterian precepts.

For the rest of his life, it was said Jackson conducted himself as a true believer, and his faith was described more uniquely his own than might be organised within the Presbyterian Church. He could never accept the idea of an "elect" chosen by God, because it offended his democratic soul.

It would have been most uncharacteristic of him to have submitted totally to all the precise teachings of the Church, but he attended services regularly and he read a portion of the Bible each day along with Biblical commentaries and the hymn book. He led family and servants in prayers at The Hermitage each night.

Jackson died of chronic tuberculosis on June 8, 1845, aged 78. His final words were: "Oh, do not cry. Be good children, and we shall all meet in heaven".

* During his period as Governor of Florida, Andrew Jackson, encouraged by his wife Rachel, clamped down on a wide range of "ungodly activity" that had been rampant then in the south-east coast community. Sabbath-breaking seemed the worst offence in Rachel's eyes and Jackson issued a decree to stop it.

Violation meant a 200 dollar fine and the posting of a 500 dollar good behaviour bond. Within a short period the draconian measures had the desired effect, with Rachel confirming: "Great order was observed; the doors kept shut; the gambling houses demolished; fiddling and dancing not heard any more on the Lord's Day; cursing not to be heard."

The Hermitage, home of President Andrew Jackson.

Distinguishing features
of the Scots-Irish

What distinguished the early immigrants was their willingness, even eagerness, to go beyond the "outer fringe of civilisation" and establish settlements on the frontier. Seaboard colonists considered the combative self-sufficient Scots-Irish the perfect Indian fighters with whom to populate their exposed borders, and evidence suggests that newly arrived immigrants were deliberately shunted there to serve as a buffer against hostile natives.

Virginia legislation decreed: "Whereas the lands . . . on the southern boundary of this colony are for the most part unseated and uncultivated; and a considerable number of persons . . . as foreign Protestants are willing to import themselves with their families and effects, and to settle upon the said lands . . . this settling of that part of the country will add to the strength and security of the colony in general."

Their experience as colonists in Ireland had made Ulstermen adaptable and assimilitive of the best traits needed for survival on the borders of America. Traditional Scotch-Irish farming, for example, emphasised slash-and-burn clearing of farms, corn-based cropping and the running of livestock in open woods - techniques well-suited to the southern backcountry.

Dr Wayne C. Moore, First Families of Tennessee
(Register of Early Settlers) 2000

2

James Robertson and John Donelson, *founders of Nashville, Tennessee*

An heroic land and river journey in the severe winter of 1779-80 which led to the founding of the city of Nashville in Tennessee was inspired by James Robertson and John Donelson, two men whose families had moved from the north of Ireland to America several generations before.

Few journeys on the American frontier can have been as perilous as the winter expedition from the Holston River in East Tennessee that led to the establishment of the Cumberland River settlement centred at Fort Nashborough (Nashville). It was a navigation exploit noted for its daring and courage and Scots-Irish families were in the frontal movement.

James Robertson - born in Brunswick county, Virginia in 1742 - was a second generation Presbyterian Ulsterman whose family had moved to North Carolina in the mid-18th century via the Shenandoah Valley of Virginia. In the early 1770s, James helped form the Watauga Association, the first white settlement in what today is North East Tennessee.

Colonel John Donelson, another Wataugan leader, was also Presbyterian of a family who moved from Gramoney in East Antrim in the early 18th century and they too arrived in North Carolina via the Shenandoah Valley. Donelson, whose daughter Rachel became the wife of Andrew Jackson, was a colonel in the Revolutionary War as well as being a builder and navigator on the great rivers of North Carolina and East Tennessee.

Moves to settle the Cumberland River territory began in 1777 in an ambitious plan drawn up by Robertson and Donelson and Richard Henderson, a North Carolina lawyer and land agent. Robertson led an exploratory team of nine to the Chickasaw Indian-populated region in 1778-79 and, after looking over the land, he reported it was time for settlement.

A 3,000-acre grant was negotiated with Henderson and arrangements made for the movement of those families who were prepared to risk all to start a new life in the far distant rugged wilderness. The journey was split up with Robertson and his 200 men and boys taking the animals (horses, cows, pigs and sheep!) and other belongings on the Kentucky route, along the Wilderness Road and through the Cumberland Gap.

Donelson and his comrades ferried the women and the children on a flotilla of small flat boats from Fort Patrick Henry along the Holston River to the Cumberland River. Because of the danger of attack from Indians, river travel was not a favoured means of communication in the Appalachian frontier region, but in the circumstances the Watauga settlers felt it was their only option.

It was an extremely cold winter - said to be the coldest in living memory in North Carolina, with the deep snow and frozen rivers making the journey for both parties almost impossible, but with dogged determination they persevered and by Christmas week of 1779 Robertson and his men had arrived at their destination. Although worn out by the rigours of the trek, they set about erecting log cabins and clearing stretches of land for the arrival of John Donelson and the families in the Spring.

The Cumberland River was frozen over and the animal stock had to be driven across the rock solid ice.

The 400-strong Donelson-piloted party, consisting mostly of women and children, left Fort Patrick Henry in an armada of 40 small flat boats and canoes and moved slowly along the Holston River. The largest boat, Adventure, had 30 families on board, including James Robertson's wife Charlotte and her five children, and Donelson's own family including Rachel (later to become Mrs Andrew Jackson!).

It was a journey into the unknown for the families; along unchartered waters, over dangerous shoals, rapids and falls, through territory where hostile Indian tribes lived and in weather conditions where only the toughest survived. After only three miles, the voyage was halted; ice and cold had set in and the frozen river made progress impossible. There was no movement until mid-February and, when the boats were eventually cut loose, they were hampered again by the swell of the river, due to incessant heavy rain.

Several boats sank and some of the voyagers took ill from smallpox and died. As they passed through the Chickamauga Indian territory the boats came under attack from tribesmen massed on the shore. There were casualties on both sides, with settlers countering the Indian assaults with sniper fire from their Kentucky long rifles.

A few boats dragged behind, some sank or fell into Indians hands, but most got through the danger point and, by the advent of Spring, they were at the mouth of the Tennessee River and the high water of the Ohio River. The flat boats were totally unsuited for the upstream currents and progress was further hampered. Supplies were also running short and it was necessary to make camp so that buffalo and bear could be hunted in the surrounding forests.

The last lap came with the journey up the Cumberland River, and on Monday April 24 the party arrived at French Salt Lick, site of present-day downtown Nashville. There was a warm welcome from James Robertson and his men, who had been toiling from Christmas to make the settlement habitable.

John Donelson recorded in his diary of April 24: "This day we arrived at our journey's end at the Big Salt Lick, where we have the pleasure of finding Captain Robertson and his company. It is a source of satisfaction to us to be enabled to restore to him and others their families who were entrusted in our care and, who some time since, perhaps, despaired of ever meeting again. Though our prospects are dreary, we have found a few log cabins which have been built on a cedar bluff above the Lick by Captain Robertson and his company."

The meandering river journey from Fort Patrick Henry to Fort Nashborough covered 985 miles, and it was a human ordeal of great magnitude for pioneers who showed remarkable spirit and endurance.

Within days, eight station settlements - scattered collections of simple log cabins, one-acre plots and fortified look-outs - were erected on the banks of the Cumberland River. Fort Nashborough was the largest, with the others Mansker's Lick, Bledsoe's, Asher's, Stone's River, Freeland's, Easton's and Fort Union. James Robertson, along with John Donelson and Richard Henderson, established the Cumberland Association, on the same lines as the Watauga Association in Tennessee in East Tennessee and again the Scots-Irish were highly influential.

Nashville soon came into being and the town expanded into the 19th century to become the leading population centre in Tennessee. While John Donelson, who died in an Indian attack in 1785, and Richard Henderson played a significant part in the founding of the city, James Robertson was acknowledged by historians as not just the "father" of Nashville, but of Tennessee.

On May 1, 1780, the settlers met and drew up the Cumberland Compact document, signed by 242 men, and set up their own government in what was a virtual wilderness. James Robertson was chosen head of the council, which administered justice, carried out regulations concerning the acquisition and transfer of lands, and acted as judge. Robertson was called upon to authorise marriages, was colonel in charge of the militia and was at the head of all the departments of government - military, legislative and judicial.

An extract from the Cumberland Compact crystallised the isolation which the Middle Tennessee settlers of 1780 found themselves in: "We are from our remote situation utterly destitute of the benefit of the laws of the country and exposed to the depredations of the Indians."

An observer of life in the Cumberland region at the time wrote: "The most unquenchable hatred existed between the Indians and the white settlers, the first struggling for their hunting grounds, the last for their lives."

Over the next two decades, the Cumberland settlement faced great danger on their frontier outpost and from constant Indian attacks, shooting, tomahawking, scalping, burning corn cribs, stealing horses and slaughtering of cattle and sheep. During the first year 60 men were killed and, in one incident, James Robertson's 13-year-old son Jonathan was wounded, scalped and left for dead. He was nursed back to a full recovery by his mother Charlotte. However, worse was to follow and in separate Indian attacks two other Robertson sons, Peyton, 12, and James Randolph, 21, were beheaded and two brothers of James, (John and Mark), killed. Robertson himself narrowly escaped death on two occasions. Once he was shot in the foot while hoeing corn and another time he was ambushed along a trail and received   gunshot wounds in both wrists.

Following these attacks, Robertson led a large expedition against the Creek Indians south of the Tennessee River and to their horror they found the scalps of white settlers killed in the Nashville area, and women who had been captured and worked as slaves on the Indian lands. Fifty Indians were killed in this 1794 expedition, and the losses forced the chieftains to engage in peace talks with the settlers.

At the height of hostilities, the Creek Indians could summon up 5,000 warriors in the region, and the Cherokees 2,000. But by the time Tennessee became a state on June 1, 1796, the worst of the Indian fighting was over.

Some of the Cumberland settlers had moved on, heading to Kentucky or to the Natchez region of Mississippi and Lousiana. During the continual fight for survival at the crucial stage of the Revolutionary War struggle and in the years following, the one man standing fearlessly was James Robertson, who, with the exception of George Washington, probably did more than anyone to defend and expand the frontier.

James Robertson, who served on the North Carolina legislature, was a Justice of the Peace and, when the first United States administration was set up, he was appointed by George Washington as brigadier general of the US Army in the territory south-west of the Ohio River, effectively the region that was to become the state of Tennessee. In 1798, he became a Tennessee senator and helped draft the first treaty of Tellico between the United States and the Cherokee Indians.

Personally, Robertson had grievously suffered from Indian attacks, but he still managed to deal fairly with the tribes in land negotiations and in re-settlements.

Robertson took care to regard the human rights of the Indians, explaining the details of treaties to them, never promising more than he believed he could achieve. The Indians said of him: "He has winning ways and makes no fuss."

During the War of 1812, Robertson was appointed Indian agent to live with the Chickasaws, to keep them friendly to the United States and prevent them from aligning with the British forces. He

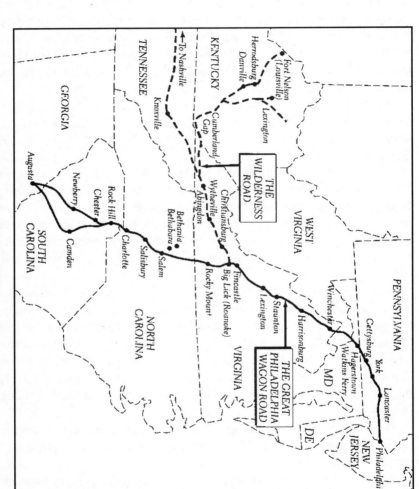

The Philadelphia Wagon Road and the Wilderness Road.

established a school for Indian children, but within two years he was taken seriously ill and died, aged 72.

Robertson was buried at the Chickasaw Agency in West Tennessee, but in 1826, by authority of the state legislature, his body was re-interred in the old city cemetery at Nashville. The cenotaph erected to his memory in Centennial Park, Nashville bears the words: "James Robertson, founder of Nashville, Pioneer, Patriot, Patriarch of Tennessee".

His wife Charlotte Reeves Robertson, the daughter of a Presbyterian minister, lived until she was 92. They had 13 children.

President Theodore Roosevelt said of James Robertson: "He belonged to a backwoods family, even poorer than the average. But he was a man of remarkable natural powers; his sombre face had in it a look of self-contained strength that made it impressive; and his taciturn, quiet, masterful way of dealing with men and affairs, together with his singular mixture of cool caution and most adventurous daring, gave him an immediate hold upon such lawless spirits as those of the border. Robertson's energy and remarkable natural ability brought him to the front, in every way."

Historian George Bancroft said: "James Robertson was my favourite hero of these times. He had self-possession, quickness of disarmament and sound judgment."

John Donelson made a significant contribution to American frontier life with the arduous 1779-80 river trek to Fort Nashborough in Middle Tennessee, but he had been an influential land speculator and and militia soldier for up to 30 years before. His father and grandfather had been involved in planting, commerce and shipping and Donelson, a highly educated man for the period, was one of the first settlers in Pittsylvania county, Virginia. He was a county surveyor and lieutenant and held the rank of colonel in the militia.

While he was involved in several military campaigns against the Overhill Cherokee Indian tribes in the Virginia-North Carolina-Tennessee region, Donelson still managed to continue dialogue with the tribes and he attended the Cherokee treaty signing at Fort Patrick Henry on the Holston River in 1777.

Donelson, a fifth signatory of the Cumberland Compact in 1780, settled with his family at the Clover Bottom site in Middle Tennessee, under cover from the nearby Mansker's Fort. But frequent attacks by Chickamauga Indians forced him to move his family to Kentucky where a close associate Daniel Boone was establishing settlements. The Donelson business contacts continued as he travelled frequently between the lands of Kentucky, Virginia and Tennessee, but in 1785 on a journey to Mansker's Fort he was fired upon and died from injuries at the Barren River. He was 67.

Andrew Jackson Donelson, a grandson of John Donelson, was aide-de-camp to his uncle Andrew Jackson during the Seminole Indian campaign and private secretary to Jackson during his political career and terms as President. In 1844 he was appointed charge d-affaires to the Texas Republic, where he successfully negotiated for annexation. He also served as minister to Prussia in 1846-49 and was an unsuccessful American Vice-President candidate for the Know-Nothing Party in 1856.

O ne of the compasses used by Colonel John Donelson on the Adventure during the 1779-80 sailing from the Holston region in East Tennessee to the Cumberland settlement is still in a good state of preservation, with its delicate mechanism unharmed. An inscription is stamped on the back: *"Made by Anthony Ham in Philadelphia for Thomas Carnahan 1755"*. A second compass, older and smaller, is broken and useless. A Fee Book, showing entries of surveys and computations made in Maryland and Virginia, as far back as 1764, has survived. Colonel Donelson began writing the diary of the Adventure voyage in the Fee Book, which was also used for logging accounts and sheds interesting light on pioneering times and customs in early Tennessee.

3

Charles Thomson, *America's first*
"Prime Minister"

Ulster-born Charles Thomson was, outside of George Washington, the most influential man in the government of America for a decade after the Revolutionary War. Thomson was secretary to the Continental Congress for 15 years from 1774 and, when the new federal constitution was adopted in 1789, he was delegated to convey to Washington at his home in Mount Vernon, Virginia the request of Congress that he become the first President.

The original Declaration of Independence of July 4, 1776 bore only two signatures, that of John Hancock, the President of Congress and Charles Thomson, the Secretary. In the political upheaval of the time, there was plenty of support for the concept of independence, but no great rush to sign the Declaration largely because of the dire consequences of failure. However, Hancock, who was also of Scots-Irish roots, and Thomson were obviously made of stern qualities, with Thomson earning the reputation of being "The Venerable Patriot".

Staunch Presbyterian Charles Thomson had moved into national politics from a classical teaching career at Philadelphia University, where he taught Latin and Greek, and, associating with the Whig movement, he espoused the politics of Benjamin Franklin, Thomas Jefferson and John Adams which increasingly pushed for American disengagement from Britain.

After Independence was declared, the four were authorised to design a seal for the new state, but six years on and the work not fulfilled, Thomson, assisted by a young Pennsylvanian lawyer William

Barton, set about the task. Within a week he had the mould of a new seal before Congress and the inscription was written into law on June 20, 1782. From Thomson's original design emerged the Great Seal of the United States of America, which since has had artistic variations and six new dies cut - in 1825, 1841, 1854, 1877, 1885 and 1904.

Charles Thomson came from a humble farming background in the Sperrin Mountains of Co Londonderry. He was born at Gorteade, Upperlands near Maghera in 1729 and his family belonged to Maghera Presbyterian Church. John and Mary Houston Thomson had six children; five sons and one daughter - William, Alexander, Charles, Matthew, John and Mary - and when his wife died at the birth of the last child, John decided on emigration to America, selling up the family farm and bidding farewell to the kinsfolk in the Maghera Church.

In 1739, the father and the five siblings set sail from Londonderry and after a rough journey across the Atlantic which took its toll on many passengers, John Thomson died of fatigue as the ship was entering Delaware Bay.

The Thomson children arrived on American soil as orphans, anguished over the tragic death of their father so soon after the loss of their mother.

Years later, Charles Thomson recalled: "I stood by the bedside of my expiring and much loved father, closed his eyes and performed the last filial duties to him." The body was buried at sea to save the cost of a land burial and, unscrupulously, the ship's captain held on to John Thomson's monies deposited in the ship's safe at the beginning of the journey.

The Thomson children found placements in Pennsylvania with family and kinsfolk and Charles started out as an apprentice black-smith. However, through the generosity of a kindly and wealthy lady, he was sent to the new classical school at Thunder Hill, New London, Pennsylvania. His tutor there was the Rev Dr Francis Allison, an Ulster Presbyterian minister from Leck outside Letterkenny in Co Donegal, and he graduated as a teacher in 1750.

Ten years later, Charles Thomson gave up teaching to develop a mercantile career and it was through his contacts in the business world of Philadelphia that he moved into politics. He was involved in treaty negotiations with the Delaware Indians and for his honesty and integrity in the dealings he was given the name "Wegh-Wu-Haw-Mo-Land", which translated means "the man who speaks the truth".

In retirement, Charles Thomson spent most of his time on translations of the Old and New Testaments of the Bible from the Greek Septuagint version. This was a quite outstanding work, but few recognised its worth at the time and regrettably after his death copies were sold as wastepaper.

Charles Thomson, whose first wife died in childbirth, died on August 16, 1824, aged 95. He was buried, as per his wish, alongside his second wife Hannah in the family plot at Harriton, Pennsylvania. The couple were later re-buried at Laurel Hill, four miles north of Philadelphia.

The Great Seal of America.

CALL MADE BY THE PEOPLE OF TEXAS!

And Resolutions adopted at the
BATTLE GROUND OF SAN JACINTO, April 21st, 1860.

The 24th Anniversary of the Battle of San Jacinto is at hand, and the friends of the HERO, who there led our troops to VICTORY, achiev-ing the Independence of Texas over the Mexican President, in person, deem the occasion a suitable one for them to assemble, not only to celebrate the great event that redeemed this fairest and best part of America, from anarchy and oppression, but to do honor to the men who there fought for our LIBERTY; and especially to vindicate the value, the genius, and patriotism of

SAM HOUSTON!

Whose military glory culminated on that battle field, and who afterwards, as President of Texas, led a new REPUBLIC through the stormy perils and vicissitude incident to the formation of government into the FAMILY OF NATIONS; moulding its institutions and directing and controlling the wild caprices of its heterogeneous population, thereby evincing to the world a capacity for statesmanship and civil administration that placed his name beside the Representative Men of the first nations of the earth.

The PEOPLE of the United States of ALL PARTIES, except the revolutionary and fanatical elements which unfortunately exist both at the North and the South, LOOK to SAM HOUSTON, as the ONLY man who has the *ability and courage* necessary to the duties that shall fall upon that man, who, as President of the United States, shall calm the troubled waters and arrest the fell spirits of disunion and fanaticism that now threaten the destruction of the Government.

The time has arrived in this history of parties and politics of this country, when only a patriot, who, like WASHINGTON and JACKSON, was never prostituted by the corruption of party, can save the nation from the perils of anarchy and civil war. Texas can, at least, offer to the *People of the Union* the NAME of SAM HOUSTON as the man for the crisis.

The undersigned, who have consulted extensively with the friends of Gen. Houston, in and out of the State, invite all who are interested, to meet at the

BATTLE GROUND OF SAN JACINTO,

On the 21st of April, instant, where every preparation will be made to entertain all who may unite to celebrate the Anniversary, or come to take counsel for the *Preservation of the Liberties* achieved on that immortal field, as well as at Bunker Hill and Yorktown, and secured to us by the *Constitution and Union of these States.*

Arrangements will be made for reduced fares on the Railroad and Steamboat routes, which will be published in due time.

A. M. GENTRY.	JOHN H. MANLY.	J. CARROL SMITH.
A. McGOWAN.	ABRAM GROESBECK,	A. S. RUTHVEN,

And hundreds of others.

THE PEOPLE'S CANDIDATE FOR PRESIDENT:

GEN. SAM HOUSTON, OF TEXAS.

FOR ELECTORS.

State at Large,		
M. T. JOHNSON, of Tarrant Co.	Eastern District.	Western District.
GEO. W. SMITH, of Jasper Co.	SAM BOGART, of Collin Co.	JESSE GRIMES, of Grimes Co.

	E. F. WILLIAMS,	ASHBEL SMITH.
	W. W. STILES.	JNO. L. BRYAN.

4

Sam Houston - *forceful individual who blazed a trail from Tennessee to Texas*

S am Houston, who boldly wrested Texas from Mexican control and was the Lone Star State's first president, and later governor when it was admitted to the Union in 1845, was the grandson of an east Co Antrim Presbyterian who emigrated to America about 1740.

This teacher-lawyer-soldier-statesmen was a forceful and courageous personality on the American frontier in the early part of the 19th century and, showing a strong streak of independence and all the traditional Scots-Irish characteristics, he blazed a trail from Tennessee to the Tex-Mex border.

The Houston (Huston) family connection can be traced back to the Ballyboley/Ballynure/Brackbracken area that lies halfway between Belfast and Larne. The Houstons were an enterprising Plantation farming family from lowland Scotland who moved into Ulster in the early 17th century.

John Houston left the port of Larne for Philadelphia with Presbyterian kinsfolk and within a few years he had reached the Shenandoah Valley of Virginia, where he was instrumental in setting up the Timber Ridge and Providence Presbyterian churches at Lexington in Rockbridge county.

Sam Houston was born at Timber Ridge on March 2, 1793, the son of Sam and Elizabeth Paxton Houston. His father Sam, a major and later colonel in the militia, was a veteran of the Revolutionary War who soldiered on the frontier until his death in 1807.

The widowed Elizabeth Paxton Houston moved with her nine children - six sons and three daughters - to Maryville, Blount county in the Great Smoky Mountain region of East Tennessee. It was a long and dangerous trek in a covered wagon through territory that skirted Cherokee Indian settlements, but Elizabeth was a determined woman, seeking a secure future for herself and young family.

She was a devout Presbyterian, described as having "intellectual gifts and strong moral qualities" above that of most women on the frontier. She led a life characterised by purity and benevolence.

Sam, in his later life, admitted his mother's wise counsel was a positive influence on him. He said: "Sages may reason and philosophers may teach, but the voice which we heard in infancy will ever come to our ears, bearing a mother's words and a mother's counsels".

The Houston home in Blount county was at Baker's Creek, a point close to the Little Tennessee River, which divided the pioneering settlements from the Cherokee Indian lands. The family enrolled at the New Providence Presbyterian Church and twice and often three times a week Elizabeth and the children walked the considerable distance over the hills to worship.

At New Providence, Sam Houston was tutored by highly respected Scots-Irish pastor the Rev Isaac Anderson, who described him as "a young man of remarkably keen and close observation". Sam was a quick learner and he soon had a firm grasp of the classics. By 18, he had graduated as a teacher and found a position at a small country school which he occupied until he was 20.

In his earlier youth, Sam Houston was attracted to the ways of the Indian tribes and he alienated his family for a period when he took up residence at a Cherokee encampment, adopting the dress and customs of the tribes and learning their language.

Soldiering was an ambition for Sam and, in 1813, he enlisted in the 7th United States Infantry for the war with the Creek Indians and in 1814 he distinguished himself at the Battle of the Horseshoe Bend. where he received three wounds - pierced in the thigh with a barbed arrow and shot twice in the right shoulder. His bravery under fire and his persistence in vigorously attacking the Creeks, even while he was severely wounded, earned respect from General Andrew Jackson, who was directing the war. The two men became firm friends and, within a year, Houston was promoted from sergeant to second lieutenant, becoming first lieutenant in 1818.

Jackson used Houston to cultivate relations with the Cherokees and his knowledge of the Indian language and culture helped him to avert a threatened uprising by tribesmen after the chiefs had surrendered a vast amount of land to the United States government. Sam later led a Cherokee delegation to Washington to receive payment for their lands and to legally settle on the bounds of their allotted reservation.

Houston resigned his army commission, after becoming dis-illusioned over allegations of complicity in the smuggling of black slaves into the United States. His position was later vindicated in a Washington inquiry and he moved to Nashville, Tennessee, where he studied law and was admitted to the bar. He, in turn, was appointed a district attorney, an adjutant general for the state of Tennessee and major-general, and in what were to be significant stepping stones to a political career Sam was elected as a Jacksonian Democrat to the United States Congress in 1823, and re-elected two years later.

He became Governor of Tennessee in 1827, and was re-elected in 1829. However, when his Presbyterian marriage to 18-year-old Flora Allen faltered after only three months, he resigned the Governorship and sought refuge with his Cherokee Indian friends, who, by this time, had been moved to Oklahoma in the Andrew Jackson-directed 'Trail of Tears' campaign.

Once again, Houston took on the dress, customs and manners of the Cherokees and hunted, fished, attended war councils and lived up to the tribes' habit for intemperance. He was even given a certificate of adoption into the Cherokee tribe and cohabited with a half-breed Indian woman Tyania Rodgers Gentry. Their association ended when she refused to desert her people on Sam's request. His own wife, a young woman of position and character in Middle Tennessee, later obtained a divorce for abandonment and she re-married. Houston was a man of varied moods and, when taken to bouts of heavy drinking, he could be a very difficult individual.

In 1833, Sam Houston headed to Texas, then in the middle of a revolution seeking to end Mexican rule. Sam was warmly welcomed by the American colonists at Nacogdoches and, adopting a hardline stance on independence for the region, he participated in the convention at San Felipe de Austin (later to become the city of Austin!), which led to the breaking of the American link.

Sam, always promoting the welfare of the native American Indians, even took part in talks with Comanche Indian chiefs on disputed boundary questions in the San Antonio region.

In the spring of 1836, Sam Houston was appointed commander-in-chief of the Texas revolutionary troops and he made the call: "Volunteers from the United States . . . come with a good rifle and come soon. Liberty or death!"

Houston was called into almost immediate action by the events that unfolded from The Alamo in San Antonio. There, Mexican President Antonio Lopez de Santa Anna and a 5,000-strong army had laid siege on 189 Texas Rangers and volunteer soldiers from Tennessee, along with a collection of women, children and black slaves. Tennessee frontiersman Davy Crockett and another Tennessean Colonel Jim Bowie, two former associates of Houston, were among those besieged at The Alamo, but reinforcements did not arrive in time and a terrible massacre occurred which stirred the American settlers in the territory.

With 700 auxiliary soldiers, hastily recruited, Sam Houston confronted Santa Anna and 1,800 Mexican troops at the Battle of San Jacinto on April 21, 1836. The odds were against them, but in 20 minutes Houston's "Texians", charging to the cry "Remember the Alamo", were victorious. The Mexicans lost 630 killed and had 730 taken prisoner, among them the hated Santa Anna, who was first to concede independence for Texas.

Sam Houston, injured in the right ankle at San Jacinto, became president of independent Texas, serving two terms - 1836-38 and 1841-44. In March, 1846 Sam was elected as a US Senator for Texas, which had been admitted to the Union four months earlier, and in this role he served 14 years.

In a speech on November 25, 1841, Sam Houston declared: "Texas has achieved her entire independence and successfully asserted her right. How has this been accomplished? By the spirit and energy of her citizens - by the valour of her sons - by the inspired language breathed by her daughters."

During his senatorship, Sam opposed the Southern state doctrine that Congress had no right to legislate on slavery in the territories. He also advocated California as a state of the Union and the development of the Pacific railroad through Texas.

In 1859, Sam was elected Governor of Texas as an Independent and he served until 1861, when on the enrolment of the state as a member of the Confederacy, he refused to take the necessary official oath and recognise the authority of the new convention.

Houston was forced out of office by Confederate politicians, but he was now an old man and war-weary, and did not resist. He wanted no more blood spilt among his own people. He retired to his farm at Huntsville and, after an illness of five weeks, died on July 26, 1863, aged 70, as the Civil War raged.

Sam married in May, 1840 to Margaret Lea, of Marion, Alabama and they enjoyed a happy stable relationship which produced eight children. Margaret was the daughter of a Baptist pastor and it was her influence which led to Sam's conversion at Independence, Texas in 1854. From being brought up in a solid Presbyterian family background where some of his close relatives were men of the cloth, Houston later experienced the heathen faiths of the Cherokees and for a brief time in Mexico Roman Catholicism. His addiction to drink did not endear him to church people during a considerable period of his career.

After his conversion to the Baptist faith, Sam regularly corresponded with his wife when away from home, providing resumes of sermons he had heard preached. He joined the Sons of Temperance organisation, leaving behind his excessive drinking habits from earlier years, but spurned a request from a delegation of Texas ministers who asked him to use his influence in getting a Sunday alcohol prohibition law passed.

After outlining his reasons, Sam added "I am a sincere Christian. I believe in the precepts and examples as taught and practised by Christ and His Apostles to be the bedrock of democracy."

He often referred to his wife Margaret as "one of the best Christians on earth" and significantly his dying words were - "Margaret, Margaret, Texas, Texas".

A newspaper report of Sam's death concluded: "To his numerous friends it will be doubtless a matter of great satisfaction to learn that in his last hours he was sustained by the Christian's hope and that he died the death of the righteous".

Sam made his will a few days before his death and in the fifth clause he said: "To my eldest son, Sam Houston, I bequeath my sword, worn in the battle of San Jacinto, to be drawn only in defence of the constitution and laws, and liberties of his country. If any attempt be made to assail one of these, I wish it to be used in its vindication".

Houston, whatever his accomplishments as a politician, statesmen and soldier, never acquired real wealth, on the level of that attained by some of his contemporaries. He was not good at finance management and, although his estate at the time of his death listed 89,288 dollars in assets, very little of this was liquid cash and his wife Margaret experienced great difficulty in making ends meet.

This fulsome tribute was paid to Sam Houston by President John F. Kennedy: "He was one of the most independent, unique, popular forceful and dramatic individuals ever to enter the Senate chamber. He was in turn magnanimous, vindictive, affectionate, yet cruel, eccentric yet self-conscious, faithful yet opportunistic. But Sam Houston's contradictions actually confirm his one basic consistent quality, indomitable individualism, sometimes spectacular, sometimes crude, sometimes mysterious, but always courageous".

Sam Houston was a man of many parts and American historian Ernest C. Shearer accurately described his moods: "He was as inconstant as a weather vane, solid as a rock, mercurial as a chameleon; intense as the heart of the sun, enthusiastic as a child, vain and proud as a peacock, humble as a servant, direct as an arrow, polished as a marquis, rough as a blizzard and gentle as a dove. In short, it was difficult to fit him to any set pattern".

* In 1850, 18,000 native Tennesseans lived in Texas, the largest contribution to the region from any other state in the Union and obviously largely due to the influence of Sam Houston and associates like Davy Crockett and Jim Bowie.

Texas became the 28th state in the Union on December 29, 1845. The Lone Star State seceded from the Union on February 23, 1861 just before the start of the Civil War, on a margin of three to one in a popular vote. The State was re-admitted to the Union in March, 1870.

5

David Crockett, *real stalwart from the Tennessee backwoods*

Brave frontiersman Davy Crockett died at The Alamo five months before his 50th birthday but in his 49 years this rugged Tennessean lived life to the full and created a legend and myth that lies at the heart of American folklore.

This highly colourful and courageous character was born in a humble log cabin in a valley alongside the Big Limestone River and the Nolichuckey River in Greene County, North Carolina (a region later to become Tennessee!) on August 17, 1786. Forget the story that Davy was born on a mountain top in Tennessee - he was born in a hollar.

Davy, who preferred to be called David, may have been a rural backwoodsman, but he had enough intelligence, commonsense and cunning to survive and outwit even his most devious adversaries and highly educated political opponents. He was in every respect a man of the people - humble, straight-talking and honest.

This fifth child of a family of nine (six sons and three daughters!), born to John and Rebecca Crockett, was a romantic adventurer, explorer and hunter who left an indelible mark on the rugged landscape of his Tennessee homeland and the stories of his exploits and achievements will always be a cornerstone of American life.

Crockett was also a soldier and politician of standing, as well as being a celebrated storyteller, folklorist and wit. He was a man with the common touch, someone who was fully aware of precisely where he had come from and where he was going.

Before spending the last few months of his life in Texas, where he stood at The Alamo stoutly defending liberty and democracy for his country, Davy lived at seven different locations in Tennessee. He spent the first twenty five years in East Tennessee; the next ten in Middle Tennessee around Nashville and the last fourteen in the wild and sparsely-inhabited West Tennessee towards Memphis.

The Crocketts had arrived in America from the north of Ireland in the early 18th century, having lived in the Tyrone-Donegal counties in the province of Ulster after moving there from Scotland during the 17th century Plantation.

Some historical records claim the family derived from French Protestant Huguenot stock (Crocketagne) and it is recorded that several Crocketts were involved in defending the Ulster city of Londonderry in the famous siege of 1688-89.

One of the first Crocketts to reach America was Joseph Louis, with his wife Sarah Stewart, from Co Donegal. These Crocketts landed in Pennsylvania, settling for a time in Maryland and then moving down the Shenandoah Valley of Virginia and further on to North Carolina, Tennessee and Missouri. Other branches of the Crockett family emigrated from Co Antrim in the 1730s.

Davy Crockett is the great grandson of Joseph Louis Crockett and his grandfather David passed through the Shenandoah Valley, verified by the fact that his son Robert was born at Barryville in the region in 1755. By 1771, the Crocketts were in North Carolina with deed records of Tryon county confirming David Sen. had bought a 250-acre farm on the south side of the Catawbe River.

In November, 1777, Davy Crockett's grandparents were massacred in a Cherokee Indian attack on their homestead at Carter's Creek beside the Holston River in Hawkins county near the present-day town of Rogersville in East Tennessee. There, within a radius of three miles David Crockett Sen. and his three sons John, William and Joseph lived on separate farmlands. Davy's father John was away at the time of the killings, but his uncle James was taken captive and did not return home for 20 years.

The massacre, marked on a gravestone in a cemetery in the centre of Rogersville, left the small clutch of Scots-Irish families in the region fearful and vulnerable, but they re-grouped to form a cohesive defensive strategy to combat the daily threat posed by Indian attack.

John Crockett took part in the Revolutionary War battles in the region, including Kings Mountain in October 1780 along with six other members of the wider family circle.

His wife Rebecca Hawkins, who was born in Maryland, also reached North Carolina via the Shenandoah Valley with her Scots-Irish family and she and John eventually settled at Limestone Creek in Greene county. Davy Crockett spent the first five years of his life at Limstone Creek. The family moved to Cove Creek where his father had a partnership in a mill, but it was a short stay as the mill and the Crockett home were destroyed in a flood. The next stop was Morristown in Jefferson county, Tennessee, where John Crockett opened a tavern on the main road from Abingdon in Virginia to Knoxville.

When he was twelve Davy was hired out as a cattle hand to a Dutch settler Jacob Silver in Rockville, Virginia. He found the work rewarding, but was homesick and trekked the 400 miles home, only to be sent back to school by his father. But the classes only lasted four days and, fearing punishment at home for his truancy, he finally decided to make his way in the wider world.

Davy tried a succession of jobs over a three-year period, and after passing through Virginia, worked for a time at Baltimore docks. He was employed by a Quaker John Kennedy, who allowed him to attend educational classes. But Davy preferred the freedom to roam the forests and mountains of his rugged and wild Tennessee homeland, as a hunter living and working off the land.

In 1806, Davy married pretty Polly Finley, who was Scots-Irish on her father's side, and, while Polly's mother was looking for better than the intrepid Crockett, the marriage blended with three children to their name, sons John Wesley and William and daughter Margaret Polly.

The couple lived for a few years on a rented farm near the home of Polly's father in Jefferson county, but the going was tough and they moved west into Middle Tennessee, beyond the Cumberland mountains. By 1811 they had settled at Mulberry Creek, on the Duck and Elk Rivers in what is now Moore county. The surrounding forests were rich in deer and smaller game, the ideal spot for a man of Davy Crockett's tastes.

Within two years Davy moved the family to Bean Creek in Franklin county, to a home called 'Kentuck' and stayed there until after his involvement in Andrew Jackson's war with the Creek Indians in 1812-14. Crockett originally volunteered for 90-day service in the Second Regiment of Volunteer Mounted Riflemen, but the military duties were extended and he was selected as a scout to spy on the Indian territories, along with a close friend George Russell. It was during this expedition that Davy gained the reputation of being a bear hunter, with his trusty Kentucky long rifle.

Davy joined the regular army and fought the Indians at Fort Strother and Fort Taladega and encountered British forces in Andrew Jackson's Florida campaign. Around this time Polly Crockett took ill at her Mulberry Creek home and Davy had to return home.

Polly had always been a delicate and frail person and the many moves and natural hardship she faced on the frontier wilderness sapped her energy and strength. She died in 1815 leaving a distraught Davy to care for three young children and, for a time, a younger brother and his wife helped out.

Within a year, Davy married again, to a widow Elizabeth Patton, the mother of two children whose husband had been killed in the Creek War. Elizabeth was also of Scots-Irish origin, of a good family background from North Carolina and her sizeable farm helped Davy to increase his social status. Elizabeth came to Texas in 1854 and died there in 1860, aged 72.

Davy, despite having taken on another wife and two more children, continued to hunt and explore and with neighbouring settlers he looked over the Alabama territory, which had just been acquired from the Creek Indians. On that mission, he contacted malaria and was fortunate to get home alive. He later took advantage of the treaty of 1816 with the Chickasaw Indians and found another settlement at Shoal Creek near Lawrenceburg in Middle Tennessee.

Within two months he was a justice of the peace and later became lieutenant colonel of the local militia.

His new found civic duties, on his own admission, were seriously taxing his educational abilities, but he claimed that he got by on his "natural born sense", rather than any knowledge of the law.

Davy was elevated to colonel in the militia and in 1821 was elected to the Tennessee state legislature for Lawrence and Hickman counties. While electioneering, he admitted he never read a newspaper and knew nothing about government, but he had talents as a soap box orator and a humour which endeared him to ordinary grassroots voters.

Crockett was also a gifted storyteller, but for all his natural instincts and talents, he was looked down on by representatives of the monied classes and slightingly referred to as "the gentleman from the cane". But Davy knew his constituency and the poor backwoods families rallied to his cause.

While attending the Tennessee legislature at Murfreesboro, Davy's large grist powder mill and distillery on Shoal Creek were swept away in a flood - a repeat of the misfortune which struck his father at Cove Creek - and he was forced to move the family to Rutherford Fork, 150 miles distance to the west. He was re-elected to the legislature in 1823, defeating Dr William E. Butler, a nephew of the wife of Andrew Jackson and one of the region's most wealthy men.

Butler had education, money and influence, but Crockett the uncanny knack of persuading voters over to his side. In his accounts, Davy tells of a special hunting shirt which he wore when campaigning. It was of buckskin, outsize and had two pockets. In one pocket, he carried whiskey and in the other tobacco.

Davy reckoned that when he met a prospective voter he would treat him first with whiskey and before leaving him he would hand him a twist of tobacco to replace the "chaw" he had disposed off when he took the drink. The reason was that if a man was in good humour, in as good a shape as when he found him, the vote was secure on polling day. Butler was routed at the polls and Crockett returned to represent five counties.

Davy Crockett was, in many respects, a socialist, although he espoused the capitalist free market ideals of the American dream. The major issue for the 1823 legislature was the disposition of lands belonging to the state and the mopping up of the territory formerly under the control of North Carolina in the late 18th century.

Crockett, who was joined by US President to be James Knox Polk in the debate, deeply mistrusted the federal government over its legislation on the territorial state remits of Tennessee and North Carolina.

Davy, who had two terms as a Tennessee state legislator, also opposed legislative handling of divorce cases and had numerous run-ins with Andrew Jackson, shortly to become President. Later, as a Congress man he irked the Washington establishment when he put forward a resolution to abolish the nation's military academy at West Point.

His main argument was that only the sons of the rich and influential could get into West Point and that the bounty of the government should go to the poor rather than to the rich. He contended that the War of 1812 had shown that a man could fight the battles of his country and lead his country's armies, without being educated at West Point; as shown by the success of Andrew Jackson who had since progressed to the highest office in the land.

In 1827 Davy was elected to Congress for West Tennessee, defeating General William Arnold and Colonel Adam Alexander, who both dismissed the Crockett bandwagon, convinced it was a straight fight between them. Davy won by 2,748 votes, and he held the seat at the next election.

However, Crockett's opposition to Andrew Jackson's Indian Bill prevented him getting a third term. Davy's attitude was: "I am at liberty to vote as my conscience and judgment dictate to be right, without the yoke of any party on me, or the driver at my heels, with the whip in his hands, commanding me 'gee-whoa-haw' just at his pleasure".

Davy was his own man, even in the presence of more auspices company, and when an usher at President Jackson's home one evening cried: "Make way for Colonel Crockett", there came the reply: "Colonel Crockett makes room for himself".

Although he fought alongside Andrew Jackson in various battles, Davy parted company with the President over land and river issues that greatly affected the livelihoods of his people. Crockett said in March, 1830: "To General Jackson I am a firm and undeviating friend. I have fought under his command . . . I have loved him . . . and still love him; but to be compelled to love everyone who . . . for self-aggrandisement pretend to rally around the 'Jackson Standard' is what I can never submit to. The people . . . ought to look for breakers! The fox is about; let the roost be guarded".

Crockett and other Tennessean representatives were disappointed at Jackson's stand against financial aid for the improvement in the transportation facilities of the state.

Davy strongly believed in human rights, including those of the native American people, and he led opposition to Andrew Jackson's Indian policy of forcing the tribes living east of the Mississippi River to move to the western part of the Louisiana territory.

When the bill approving the measure at a cost of 500,000 dollars was put before Congress in 1830, Davy was the only Tennessean to vote against it. His main objective was that he did not want to see the poor remnants of "a once powerful people" forced to move "against their will".

Davy represented four counties in West Tennessee on the border of the Chickasaw Indian country and he was appalled at the decision to drive these tribes west of the Mississippi. He also knew that many by now-peaceful Cherokees would prefer "death in their homes" to moving away from their natural environment in Tennessee.

During his last term in Congress, Davy toured major eastern cities and New England states and, wherever he went, he was met by huge crowds and great ovations.

Davy was in big demand as a speaker at banquets and dinner parties and when he visited Philadelphia he was presented with his famous rifle 'Betsy'. This bore the gold and silver inscription: "To the honourable Davy Crockett of Tennessee by the young men of Philadelphia".

'Betsy' was to accompany Davy on his last fateful journey to Texas for the battles with the Mexicans - and, nostalgically, the trusted weapon was recovered by his family after the fall at The Alamo.

Spreading the Word

Robert Aitken (1734-1802), a Quaker who left Ireland because of religious persecution and settled in Pennsylvania, was responsible for the publication of 30,000 Bibles in America in 1781 at a cost of 10,000 dollars. Aitken was given approval and financial aid by the United States Congress after he had lodged a petition, in violation of English law. He played a leading role in the Revolutionary War.

"My Ulster blood is my most priceless heritage."

President James Buchanan,
son of James Buchanan from Co. Tyrone.

6

The Crockett Trail *to Texas and The Alamo*

D avy Crockett left his West Tennessee home for Texas on November 1, 1835, three months after his election defeat for Congress. His political career was over and the tremendous urge to explore new territory had again seized him. His aim was to improve his economic well-being on the Texas frontier. He told contemporaries: "You can go to hell, I'm going to Texas".

Davy moved to Texas down the Mississippi River through Arkansas and into the Red River Valley. This verged on Comanche Indian country where the tribes were on the warpath, as menacing to the American settlers as the Mexicans under their President, General Antonio Lopez de Santa Anna.

Soon after his arrival in Nacogdoches, Davy took the oath of allegiance to the provisional government of the independent republic of Texas. He was joined by his nephew William Patton, who had accompanied him to Texas in an initial 17-strong party which was to be become known as the "Tennessee Mounted Volunteers".

Texas was in revolt against the ruling junta in Mexico and the stakes were high as both sides prepared for a fight to the death. Crockett and his men reported for duty at Bexar on January 13, 1836 and they were warmly welcomed by Colonel William Travis, who, because Crockett also bore the title of Colonel, offered him command of the fort. Crockett refused, stating he had come to defend Texas as a humble private.

When word came through on February 11 that Santa Anna and a large army had crossed the Rio Grande into Texas, it was decided that all the men of the Texas garrison should go as soon as possible into the enclosure of The Alamo, an old walled Franciscan mission station in what today is the centre of the city of San Antonio.

The movement into The Alamo was not completed until February 23 and it was there over the next two weeks that 189 men, together with some women, children and black servants, were to take refuge from the advancing 5,000-strong Mexican army led by Santa Anna.

Most of the volunteers including Crockett, were Tennesseans; the rest were Kentuckians and Virginians. Among them was a Tennessean of Scottish roots, Colonel Jim Bowie, the man credited with inventing the Bowie knife. Illness from tuberculosis prevented Jim from taking an active role in the battle. Colonel William Travis, aged only 25, was in command and he kept repeating even at the height of battle: "Victory or death! I shall never surrender or retreat!"

Sam Houston, like Crockett of Ulster-Scots extraction, was major-general of the regular army in the new independent republic of Texas, but it was an army which had still to be recruited. The siege lasted 13 days and, while guns were fired daily at sunrise to alert army reinforcements, it was to no avail.

The siege began on February 23, 1836 and Crockett's pledge to Colonel Travis was "Colonel, here I am. Assign me a position and I and my boys will try to defend it". The "boys " were the Tennesseans and they were assigned to the most vulnerable point at the station.

In a memorandum dated February 23, Crockett wrote: "Early this morning the enemy came in sight, marching in regular order. They'll find that they have to do with men who will never lay down their arms as long as they can stand on their legs". Ominously, in another record-ed message on March 3, Crockett declared: "We have given over all hope of receiving assistance from Goliad or Refugio".

Eighteen cannon were mounted as the siege began and Travis in his report said: "The Hon. David Crockett was seen at all points animating the men to do their duty". The accurate rifle fire of the Tennesseans kept the Mexicans at bay, but time and supplies were running out. And there was no sign of the army reinforcements that had been promised.

A detachment of 32 men arrived on March 1, but two days later there came the news from a courier that 400 men had turned back because of difficulties on the way and, because the officers felt another Texas station was more in need of defending than The Alamo.

Santa Anna decided the fort should be taken by assault and the first two charges were beaten back with huge losses on the part of the Mexicans. In a third assault, concentrating on the north wall of the fort, the Mexicans managed to breach the defences and gain access to the plaza of the mission.

The Texans were outnumbered and had to retreat to the buildings around the plaza and the mission church. Their cannons were seized and used to batter down the doors. The defenders took their last stand in hand-to-hand combat and many died at the receiving end of a Mexican bayonet.

An estimated 189 Texans were killed, with their bodies placed on a funeral pyre and burned. The only survivors were non-combatants, mostly Mexican women and children, several black slaves of Colonel Bowie and Colonel Travis, and a Mrs Dickinson, the wife of an officer of the garrison.

Various accounts of how Davy Crockett died at the Alamo have been rendered. It is claimed he was one of six survivors who surrendered to Santa Anna and was shot dead on the Mexican leader's orders. But is is generally accepted that he fell behind the south wall, which he and the Tennesseans were charged to defend. Mrs Dickinson, who was led from the church, said in her testimony: "As we passed through the enclosed ground in front of the church I saw heaps of dead and dying. I recognised Colonel Crockett lying dead and mutilated between the church and the barrack building and even remember seeing his peculiar cap lying by his side".

Two slave witnesses, Santa Anna's cook Ben and Colonel Travis's servant Joe, claimed Crockett's body was surrounded by Mexican corpses. Ben reported seeing Davy's knife buried "up the hilt in the bosom of a Mexican found lying across his body". It was said that Crockett fought to the end, killing many Mexicans. His last act of helpfulness was loading Jim Bowie's rifle and pistol.

General Sam Houston found the fall of The Alamo an agonising nightmare. Ironically, Sam was presiding at a convention in

Washington dealing with the independence of Texas and, when word reached him of the last message ever dispatched by Colonel Travis, he walked out, mounted his battle horse and, with three companions, headed for The Alamo.

The party rode hard all day, only stopping when their wearied horses could go no further. He knew that the signal gun would be fired as long as The Alamo held out. The last one was fired on the day that he had read Travis's message (Sunday March 6) - the day the Mexicans butchered the last of the 189 men. Sam Houston was too late to render assistance at The Alamo, but through his leadership, and, against all the odds, he managed to retrieve the position for the Texan cause in the days that followed.

The Alamo, by tieing down Santa Anna's army for two weeks, had allowed the Texan army to get organised. The battle cry had now become "Remember The Alamo" and, under Houston, the Texans, heavily outnumbered but determined to "save Texas", won a famous victory at the Battle of San Jacinto. It was 700 brave, but largely untrained Texas against 1,800 Mexicans, and, buoyed by the frenzied cries of "The Alamo", Houston's men won the day in 20 minutes.

The Mexicans had 630 killed and 730 prisoners were taken, including their commander Santa Anna. The Texan losses were eight killed and 23 injured.

Houston, who suffered an ankle injury, secured from Santa Anna a treaty recognising Texas independence and, by September of that year, he was President of the new republic. Texas later became a State of the Union - the 28th- on December 29, 1845.

The Telegraph and Texas Register in Austin reported in its issue of March 24, 1836: "The end of Davy Crockett of Tennessee, the great hunter of the west, was as glorious as his career through life had been useful. He and his companions were found surrounded by piles of assailants, whom they immolated on the altar of Texas liberties. The countenance of Crockett was unchanged: he had in death that freshness of hue, which his exercise of pursuing the beasts of the forest and the prairie had imparted to him. Texas places him, exultingly, amongst the martyrs of her cause".

John Wesley Crockett, Davy's son, who later represented his father's old constituency of West Tennessee in the American

Congress, wrote to his uncle George Patton, of North Carolina: "You have doubtless seen the account of my father's fall at the Alamo in Texas. He is gone from us and is no more to be seen in the walks of men, but in his death like Sampson (Samson) he slew more of his enemies than in all of his life. Even his most bitter enemies here, I believe, have buried all animosity and joined the great lamentation over his untimely death".

Davy's last reported memorandum, written on March 5, carried the words: Go ahead, liberty and independence forever!"

Some military strategists may look back on The Alamo as a disaster - that a body of soldiers was allowed to be surrounded by a force vastly superior in numbers, but it is widely accepted that the supreme sacrifice made by Davy Crockett and the others in the little mission station largely contributed to securing independence for Texas.

Shortly after The Alamo, John Wesley Crockett went to Texas to retrieve his father's rifle 'Betsy' and, with other personal belongings, the weapon became a treasured possession in the family, being handed down from generation to generation. Davy Crockett once wrote: "I'll leave the truth for others when I'm dead. First be sure you are right and go ahead".

James Wakefield Burke, in his book David Crockett - the man Behind the Myth, wrote of the legendary Tennessean: "David Crockett possessed the essential attributes for the American frontier. He was an adventurer, with a talent for falling in with strangers, a memory for names and faces, a gift of storytelling, inexhaustible invention, indomitable valiance, a remarkable ability for sharp-shooting and that freedom from conscience that springs from a contempt for pettiness and bureaucracy.

"He was a free soul who sought the company only of those of like temperament. There seems to have been graven into this liberated man from the dirt farms of Tennessee a reluctance to be tied down, to be obligated for long to any engagement, to own anything save his long rifle".

Obviously this was a man in the highest traditions of his Scots-Irish family heritage. The legend and myth of Davy Crockett was indeed real, not imaginary.

The Alamo

7

Roll of honour *for the brave "Texian" heroes of The Alamo*

One hundred and eighty nine men, mostly Texans and Tennesseans, died at The Alamo died in March, 1836 fighting for the freedom and liberty of Texas. Nine of those killed were born in Ireland, mostly in Ulster, and many others like Davy Crockett were first, second or third generation away from Scots-Irish pioneering settlers who crossed the Atlantic on the immigrant ships.

One of the fallen heroes, Kentuckian Daniel William Cloud, proclaimed on December 26, 1835 en route to the Alamo: "If we succeed, the Country is ours. It is immense in extent and fertile in its soil and will amply reward all our toil. If we fail, death in the cause of liberty and humanity is not cause for shuddering. Our rifles are by our side, and choice guns they are, we know what awaits us and are prepared to meet it."

Earlier on December 5-10, the "Texians" won a significant victory with the storming of San Antonio in what became known as the Siege of Bexar. The stand by the vastly outnumbered "Texians" managed to impede the progress of Santa Anna and his Mexican army and allowed more time to prepare for the difficult days ahead.

In fierce hand to hand fighting over five days in the Siege of Bexar, the "Texians", led by Benjamin Rush Milam, forced Mexican troops from their strategic positions in San Antonio. The victorious volunteers then occupied the old mission station at The Alamo for what was to be an eventful three months.

The siege of The Alamo started on February 23, 1836 when 5,000 Mexican troops led by General Antonio Lopez de Santa Anna surrounded the mission station bravely manned by the defenders under the command of Colonel William Travis.

On the eighth day of the siege, 32 volunteers from Gonzales arrived, bringing the number of defenders to nearly 200. But Colonel Travis, realising that the possibility of recruiting additional manpower was fading, drew a line on the ground and asked any man willing to stay on and fight to step over. All except one did.

The defenders saw The Alamo as the key to the defence of Texas and their independence and they were ready to give their lives rather than surrender their position to Santa Anna. The odds were stacked against them, but they considered it was their duty to stand and fight.

The 13-day siege ended at sunrise on March 6 when the Mexicans mounted the walls in desperate hand-to-hand combat and, after overwhelming the Texans by sheer numbers, rushed the compound and seized control of the station.

The Alamo is situated in the centre of San Antonio, the third largest city in Texas today. Strong Mexican and Spanish influences in character and language remain in San Antonio today and the revered Alamo site is the mecca for millions of tourists every year.

San Antonio, a region once inhabited by Indian tribes, was founded as a Spanish mission in 1718, named after their patron saint St Anthony of Padua, and the city grew to become the capital of the Spanish Empire's northern territories in the New World. The city was the scene of Mexican revolts against the Spanish, and later between Mexico and Americans fighting for their independence.

The 189 heroes, listed by the Daughters of the Republic of Texas as gallantly laying down their lives on the Texan side, are:

A   Juan Abamillo (born San Antonio, Texas), Robert Allen (unknown), Miles DeForest Andross (unknown), Micajah Autry (born North Carolina).

B   Juan A. Badillo (born San Antonio, Texas), Peter James Bailey (born Kentucky), Isaac G. Baker (born Arkansas), William Charles M. Baker (born Kentucky), John J. Ballentine (unknown),

Richard W. Ballentine (born Scotland), John J. Baugh (born Virginia), Joseph Bayliss (born Tennessee), John Blair (born Tennessee), Samuel B. Blair (born Tennessee), William Blazeby (born England), James Butler Bonham (born South Carolina), Daniel Bourne (born England), James Bowie (born Tennessee), Jesse B. Bowman (unknown), George Brown (born England), James Brown (born Pennsylvania), Robert Brown (unknown), James Buchanan (born Alabama), Samuel E. Burns (born Ireland), George D. Butler (born Missouri).

C   Robert Campbell (born Tennessee), John Cain (born Pennsylvania), William R. Carey (born Maryland), Charles Henry Clark (born Missouri), M. B. Clark (unknown), Daniel William Cloud (born Kentucky), Robert E. Cochran ((born New Jersey), George Washington Cottle (born Tennessee), Henry Courtman (born Germany), Lemuel Crawford (born South Carolina), David Crockett (born Tennessee), Robert Crossman (born Massachusetts), David P. Cummings (born Pennsylvania), Robert Cunningham (born New York).

D   Jacob C. Darst (born Kentucky), John Davis (born Kentucky), Freeman H. K. Day (unknown), Jerry C. Day (born Missouri), Squire Daymon (born Tennessee), William Dearduff (born Tennessee), Stephen Dennison (born England), Charles Despallier (born Louisiana), Almaron Dickinson (born Tennessee), John H. Dillard (born Tennessee), James R. Dimpkins (born Tennessee), Lewis Dewall (born New York), Andrew Duvalt (born Ireland).

E   Carlos Espalier (born San Antonio, Texas), Gregorio Esparza (born San Antonio, Texas), Robert Evans (born Ireland), Samuel B. Evans (born Kentucky), James I. Ewing (born Tennessee).

F   William Fishbaugh (born Alabama), John Flanders (born Massachusetts), Dolphin Ward Floyd (born North Carolina), John Hubbard Forsyth (born New York), Antonio Fuentes (born San Antonio Texas), Galba Fugua (born Gonzales, Texas), William K. Furtleroy (born Kentucky).

G   William Garnett (born Tennessee), James W. Garrand (born Louisiana), James Girard Garrett (born Tennessee), John E. Garvin (unknown), John E. Gaston (born Kentucky), James George (unknown), John Calvin Goodrich (born Tennessee), Albert Calvin Grimes (born Georgia), Jose Maria Guerrero (born Laredo, Texas), James C. Gwynne (born England).

H   James Hannum (unknown), John Harris (born Kentucky), Andrew Jackson Harrison (unknown), William B. Harrison (born Ohio), Charles M. Heiskell (born Tennessee), Joseph B. Hawkins (born Ireland), John M. Hays (born (born Tennessee), Patrick Henry Herndon (born Virginia), William Daniel Hersee (England), Tapley Holland (unknown), Samuel Holloway (born Pennsylvania), William D. Howell (born Massachusetts).

J   William Daniel Jackson (born Ireland), Thomas Jackson (born Kentucky), Green B. Jameson (born Kentucky), Gordon C. Jennings (born Connecticut), Jimenes (Ximenes) (Texas), Lewis Johnson (born Wales), William Johnson (born Pennsylvania), John Jones (born New York).

K   Johnnie Kellog (unknown), James Kenney (born Virginia), Andrew Kent (born Kentucky), Joseph Kerr (born Louisiana), George C. Kimbell (born New York), William P. King (Texas).

L   William Irvine Lewis (born Virginia), William J. Lightfoot (born Virginia), Jonathan J. Lindley (born Illinois), William Linn (born Massachusetts), Toribio D. Losoya (born San Antonio, Texas).

McC Edward McCafferty (unknown), Jesse McCoy (Tennessee), William McDowell (born Pennsylvania), James McGee (born Ireland), Robert McGregor (born Scotland), Robert McKinney (born Tennessee).

M   George Washington Main (born Virginia), William T. Malone (born Georgia), William T. Marshall (born Tennessee), Albert

Martin (born Tennessee), Eliel Melton (born Georgia), Thomas R. Miller (born Virginia), William Mills (born Tennessee), Isaac Millsaps (born Mississippi), Edward F. Mitchusson (born Virginia), Napoleon B. Mitchell (unknown), Edwin T. Mitchell (unknown), Robert B. Moore (born Virginia), Willis Moore (born Mississippi), Robert Musselman (born Ohio).

N   Andres Nava (born San Antonio, Texas), George Neggan (born South Carolina), Andrew W. Nelson (born Tennessee), Edward Nelson (born South Carolina), George Nelson (born South Carolina), James Northcross (born Virginia), James Nowlan (born England).

P   George Pagan (born Mississippi), Christopher Parker (born Mississippi), William Parks (North Carolina), Richardson Perry (born Texas), Amos Pollard (born Massachusetts).

R   John Purdy Reynolds (born Pennsylvania), Thomas H. Roberts (unknown), Isaac Robinson (born Scotland), James Robertson (born Tennessee), James M. Rose (born Virginia), Jackson J. Rusk (born Ireland), Joseph Rutherford (born Kentucky), Isaac Ryan (born Louisiana).

S   Mial Scurlock (born North Carolina), Marcus J. Sewell (born England), Manson Shied (born Georgia), Cleveland Kinlock Simmons (born South Carolina), Andrew H. Smith (born Tennessee), Charles S. Smith (born Maryland), Joshua G. Smith (born North Carolina), William H. Smith (unknown), Richard Starr (born England), James E. Stewart (born England), Richard L. Stockton (born Virginia), A. Spain Summerlin (born Tennessee), William E. Summers (born Tennessee), William D. Sutherland (born Alabama).

T   Edward Taylor (unknown), George Taylor (unknown), James Taylor (unknown), William Taylor (born Tennessee), B. Archer M. Thomas (born Kentucky), Henry Thomas (born Germany), Jesse G. Thompson (born Arkansas), John W. Thompson (born

North Carolina), John M. Truston (born Pennsylvania), Burke Trammel (born Ireland), William Barrett Travis (born South Carolina), George W. Tumlinson (born Missouri), James Tylee (born New York), John (negro - unknown).

W Asa Walker (unknown), Jacob Walker (unknown), William B. Ward (born Ireland), Henry Warnell (born Arkansas), Joseph G. Washington (born Tennessee), Thomas Waters (born England), William Wells (born Georgia), Isaac White (born Kentucky), Robert White (unknown), Hiram J. Williamson (born Pennslyvania), William Wills (unknown), David J. Wilson (born Scotland), John Wilson (born Pennslyvania), Anthony Wolfe (born England), Claiborne Wright (born North Carolina).

Z Charles Zanco (born Denmark).

The Appeal sent by Colonel William Barrett Travis from The Alamo on February 24, 1836

To the people of Texas and all Americans in the world; Fellow Citizens and compatriots,

I am besieged by a thousand or more of the Mexicans under Santa Anna. I have sustained a continual bombardment and cannonade for 24 hours and have not lost a man. The enemy has demanded our surrender at discretion, otherwise the garrison are to be put to the sword if the fort is taken. I have answered the demand with a cannon-shot and our flag still waves proudly from the walls. I shall never surrender or retreat. Then I call upon you in the name of Liberty, of patriotism, and everything dear to the American character, to come to our aid with all dispatch. The enemy is receiving reinforcements daily and will no doubt increase to three or four thousand in four or five days. If this call is neglected I am determined to maintain myself as long as possible and die like a soldier who never forgets what is due to his own honor and that of his country.

Victory or death.

William Barrett Travis

8

Irishmen and Scots-Irish descendants
who died at The Alamo

SAMUEL BURNS. Aged 26. Born Ireland and lived at Natchitoches, Louisiana. He moved to Texas at the start of the hostilities with Mexico and was an artilleryman in Captain Carey's artillery company.

ANDREW DUVALT (DEVAULT). Aged 32. A native of Ireland, Duvalt lived at Gonzales, Texas, and was a plasterer by trade. He was a rifleman in Captain White's infantry company and came to Texas from Missouri. Took part in the battle of Bexar and received a donation of 640 acres of lands for his service. Some time after February 2, 1836, he returned to Gonzales and mustered with the Gonzales Ranging Company before heading to The Alamo,

ROBERT EVANS. Aged 36. Major Robert Evans, an impressive six feet tall soldier, was the master of ordinance at The Alamo and the last soldier to die in the siege. Evans had moved from Ireland to New York and made it to Texas via New Orleans. During the final moments at The Alamo on March 6, 1836, he tried to explode the several hundred pounds of powder in the magazine at the monks' burial room as the Mexican forces overpowered the hopelessly outnumbered Texas garrison. Already wounded and by then the last Texas survivor, Evans was shot by a Mexican officer and fell with his torch only about a foot away from the powder train. Reports indicate Santa Anna, the Mexican general, was in the room at the time and folklore has it he stabbed the dying Evans twice in the breast with his sword.

JOSEPH MARK HAWKINS. Aged 37. Born Ireland. Came to Texas by way of Louisiana. Was a private rifleman and is thought to have been one of the volunteers who followed Jim Bowie to the battle of Bexar and The Alamo.   Was originally from Virginia. A letter of January 20, 1836, bearing his signature, shows he was a man of intelligence and influence.

THOMAS JACKSON. Aged 32. Born in Ireland, Thomas lived at Gonzales, Texas after moving down from Kentucky where his Scots-Irish immigrant family had settled. A brother-in-law was Tennessee George Washington Cottle, who was also killed at The Alamo

JAMES McGEE. A native of Ireland and a private in Captain Blazeby's infantry company, James was a resident of Gonzales, Texas after coming to the state by way of New Orleans. He took part in the battle of Bexar and was wounded during the initial storming of The Alamo. He died on March 3, 1836.

JACKSON J. RUSK. Born in the north of Ireland. A rifleman private in Captain Baker's company, Rusk may have been one of the volunteers who accompanied Jim Bowie to Bexar and The Alamo. He had no heirs who claimed land entitled to him after his death. This was most unusual for in most cases relatives had requested land for services of deceased men. It can be presumed that Jackson J. Rusk's family never knew he died fighting at The Alamo.

BURKE TRAMMEL. Aged 26, Born in Ireland, Trammel came to Texas from Tennessee as one of Davy Crockett's companions to serve in Captain Carey's artillery company. He was allocated 640 acres for his part in the battle of Bexar. The muster rolls at The Alamo show that Trammel signed as "Tommel". His heirs received 1,920 acres of land in Texas.

WILLIAM B. WARD. Aged 30. William B. was a drum sergeant who was born in the south of Ireland. He is believed to have in the British Army, probably in the Royal Fusiliers, and served in India before emigrating to America. He came to Texas from New Orleans, but it is uncertain as to what military unit he belonged to at the siege. When the Mexicans appeared first on the scene and the Texans returned to The Alamo, Ward was seen in an artillery position covering the main gate to the mission post. Ward was a man known to take drink, but, significantly on this occasion, his demeanour was described as sober and calm - "the only man who knew what to do at the time".

•••

ROBERT CAMPBELL. Age 26, Campbell, of a strong Scots-Irish family, came to Texas via Tennessee in January, 1836 and served as a lieutenant in Captain Harrison's company.

WILLIAM DANIEL JACKSON. Age 29. A Kentuckian from a Scots-Irish family, Jackson was an artilleryman in Captain Carey's artillery company. He also took part in the siege and battle of Bexar.

JESSE McCOY. Aged 32. The son of Scots-Irish parents John and Martha McCoy, Jesse was born at Gyrosburg, Tennessee. A town sheriff in Gonzales, Texas, he arrived in Texas from Missouri in 1827 and on February 23 was mustered as a rifleman private in the Gonzales Ranging Company. He entered The Alamo with his unit on March 1, 1836.

WILLIAM McDOWELL. Aged 43. Born Mifflin county, Pennsylvania. A resident of Tennessee, William was a rifleman in Captain Harrison's company. The son of Scots-Irish militia man Colonel John McDowell, of Kishacoguillas Valley, Pennsylvania, he left Tennesseee for Texas in 1835 and was sworn into the Volunteer Auxiliary Corps of Texas at Nacogdoches on January 14, 1836. He rode to Bexar and The Alamo as a member of Captain Harrison's company, arriving there about February 9, 1836.

ROBERT McKINNEY. Aged 27. This Tennessean of Scots-Irish descent came to Texas via New York and New Orleans.

JAMES ROBERTSON. This son of Felix and Lydia Waters Robertson, a prominent Scots-Irish family in Tennessee, came to Texas from Louisiana and served as a private under Davy Crockett at The Alamo. Robertson, married to a Sarah Carson, was the grandson of Colonel James Robertson, a leader of the Watauga community in East Tennessee during the 1770s and founder of Nashville (Fort Nashborough) in 1780.

Fall of The Alamo (painting by Theodore Gentilz (1819-1906).

9

William Irvine Lewis - *Alamo victim with Ulster links on two sides of his family*

William Irvine Lewis, great grandson of Donegal-born John Lewis, the first Scots-Irish Presbyterian to settle in the Shenandoah Valley of Virginia in 1732, died alongside Davy Crockett at The Alamo. He was 28.

Virginia-born William Irvine Lewis, son of Dr Charles W. and Mary Bullen Irvine Lewis, moved to Texas from Pennsylvania via North Carolina and he served as a rifleman private attached to the Tennessee Mountain Volunteers (Davy Crockett's men!).

Lewis's mother, whose Ulster-born father William Irvine was a brigadier general in Pennsylvania, wrote to the Telegraph and Texas Register in October, 1840 requesting for a memento of her son. A small monument carved from a stone from The Alamo ruins was sent to her.

The Bible belonging to William Irvine Lewis was a memento left behind at The Alamo. It had been presented to him by his grandfather William Lewis as he lay on his death bed, having been brought from Ireland when John Lewis moved in 1732. The Bible was printed in Dublin and bears the British Royal Coat of Arms.

The heirs of William Irvine Lewis received 1920 acres of land for his service in Texas. Lewis's Donegal-born grandfather William developed mineral deposits in West Virginia and the Lewis family had a distinguished line of soldiering through the Revolutionary War, the Indian frontier campaigns and the American Civil War.

A brother of William Irvine Lewis, Armstrong Irvine Lewis, was a captain in the Texas navy before annexation; a cousin Callender Irvine Fayssoux was the youngest midshipman in the Texas navy, and another cousin 19-year-old Armstrong Irvine Fayssoux was killed at Buena Vista fighting in a Mississippi regiment under Jefferson Davis in the Mexican War.

Brigadier General William Irvine, William Irvine Lewis's grandfather, was born near Enniskillen in Co Fermanagh in 1741 and, after graduating from Trinity College in Dublin, he served as a soldier in the British army and as a surgeon on a British war ship during the Seven Years War. By 1764, Irvine was a doctor at Carlisle in Pennsylvania and there he married Anne Callender, daughter of Captain Robert Callender, another Scots-Irishman. They had eleven children, five sons and six daughters.

Irvine was a member of the provincial convention in Philadelphia of July 15, 1774, which denounced British "tyranny" in Boston and he loudly declared for American rights. He raised and commanded the 6th Pennsylvania Regiment during the Revolutionary War and was involved in expeditions to Canada, and was also based at Fort Pitt (Pittsburgh), fending off numerous Indian raids.

After the war, William Irvine wrote to George Washington, with whom he was very closely associated, both personally and professionally, complementing the General on his success. Washington replied: "With great sincerity, I return you my congratulations". Irvine was rewarded with a very generous land grant in Pennsylvania and he was appointed agent to administer the land grants allocated to the troops. In 1790, Irvine served on the Pennsylvanian constitutional convention and in 1794 he acted as arbitrator and commanding officer of the state troops in quelling the whiskey rebellion in Western Pennsylvania, involving the Scots-Irish settlers. He died in Pennsylvania in 1804.

10

Christopher Parker - *young man destined to die at The Alamo*

C hristopher Adams Parker, a prosperous young man of Scots-Irish roots, filed his will eighteen months before dying at The Alamo. We will never know whether it was premonition that persuaded this brave 20-year-old volunteer to name his father William as his heir, but obviously he was acutely aware of the dangerous climate existing in the Texan-Mexican conflict of the time and knew death could come at any time.

Texas and the conflict between Protestant Anglo-Americans and Roman Catholic Mexicans had caught the imagination of many individuals throughout the United States, especially in the South. Christopher Parker was one of them.

Soldiering was a family tradition for Christopher Parker; Virginian James Armstrong, his grandfather on his mother Hannah's side, stood with General George Washington at Valley Forge during the Revolutionary War, and his own father William fought with Andrew Jackson at the Battle of New Orleans in 1815.

William Parker and his wife owned the Mississippi Hotel at Natchez, Mississippi, a region settled by Scots-Irish families from about 1780 into the early 19th century. The hotel, elegant three-storey premises, offered "probably the best accommodation to be had in Natchez" and the couple had two children - Christopher Adams and a daughter Minerva.

Christopher was given a classical education at Boston, Massachusetts and, moving from his youth into adulthood, he was to acquire considerable wealth and property, largely as a result of his father's influence at Natchez. He resided for a time in New Orleans, Louisiana and in 1834 he and his sister Minerva inherited their shares of the Mississippi Hotel, which had been held in trust for them from childhood. It was about this time that Christopher filed his personal hand-written will, naming his "dearly beloved father" William as his sole heir and the one to pay his debts and have his body buried.

Early in 1835, Christopher bought his sister's share in the hotel for 8,000 dollars, but tales told by travellers on the Mississippi River about the expansion of the frontier in the deep South caught the young Parker's imagination and in November, 1835 he moved down to Texas from the Natchez region, registering for military service as a private in Vehlein's Colony.

A month later at Goliad, Christopher signed the first Texas Declaration of Independence, and, although little is known of his movements between December, 1835 and February 1836, he did spend the last 13 fateful days of his life holed up at the fortress station of The Alamo.

Minerva Parker married Edward Sparrow, a business associate of Christopher in Natchez, and the couple, who had three daughters, lived in Vidalia, Louisiana after moving from Mississippi. Edward Sparrow, of an Anglo-Irish family of Quakers who had settled in Ireland in the 17th century English plantation years, sponsored a group of volunteers from the region to Texas to fight in the 1845 war against the Mexicans at the time Texas became a state of the Union.

The volunteers, recruited from the Montezuma regiment, fought to keep navigation open on the Rio Grande river and, when hostilities ended in August, 1846, they returned to resume their lives and work in Vidalia.

For most of 50 years from the late 18th century, the southern territories running into Mexico was a region of fierce conflict over disputed land and sovereignty by Spanish Americans, Indians and European ethnic groups who had settled the Appalachian states. By 1825, Mexico had established a liberal constitution, but the promise was not fulfilled, and despots ruled as Mexico's imperial dreams were shattered in losses to Anglo-America beginning after The Alamo in 1836.

In the course of time all territories north of the Rio Grande were captured as spoils of war or ceded through territory to the United States. Louisiana, Mexico's neighbour to the east, was already incorporated into America by 1825. Thomas Jefferson's insight and selectively loose interpretation of the American Constitution sealed the purchase of the extensive Louisiana territories from the French.

Texas and Louisiana played a pivotal role in the United States's economic expansion of the mid-19th century. Railroads criss-crossed the states enabling cotton farmers and cattle ranchers to gain access to markets. Steamships called at Lake Providence, Louisiana on their way to New Orleans, and both Texas and Louisiana were connected by sea routes to New York, Mobile, Pensacola, Tallahassee, Tampa, Key West and Havana

During the American Civil War, Edward Sparrow served the Confederacy in Richmond, Virginia as Louisiana's senator, was chairman of the Confederate military committee and signed the Declaration for Secession of Louisiana from the Union. However, when the Union forces triumphed he and his wife Minerva urged their neighbours and Confederate sympathisers to accept defeat pragmatically, and continue with the business of living. To that end, Edward arranged for the importation of Irish labourers to replace the Black slaves as a source of plantation labour.

In 1871, the couple deeded three lots on their Arlington plantation to the Grace Episcopal Church to "advance the principles of religion" and the interests of that denomination. Steamboats ferried the building materials for the church from New Orleans and "a large, roomy and walnut interior building" was erected.

In 1896, the Sparrow-Parker families linked up with the Wylys, another Scots-Irish family, when Mary Decker, grand-daughter of Edward and Minerva Sparrow, married Charles Samuel Wyly, an attorney in Louisiana.

Charles Samuel was the great grandson of late 18th century Scots-Irish Presbyterian pastor the Rev Hazekiah Balch, founder of Tusculum College at Greeneville in East Tennessee. Samuel Young Wyly, Charles Samuel's father, was also a Presbyterian minister educated at Princeton theological seminary.

The Wylys, a family who contributed much to the independence, spiritual and intellectual growth of America during their North Carolina, Tennessee and Texas settlements, were also connected to the Kelleys, who arrived from Ireland in 1664, settling first in New Jersey and moving over a period of time to Ohio and Louisiana; and the Evans family, who moved from South Carolina to Mississippi and Lousiania. Major John Kelley led the New Jersey state militia in the Revolutionary War.

* Hezakiah Benjamin Balch, believed to be a son of the East Tennessee pastor, is listed as having fought at the battle of San Jacinto in Texas on April 21, 1836, in which a Sam Houston-led Texan army routed the Mexican forces led by Santa Anna.

This surveyor's map - dating from sometime just before 1791 - shows the boundaries of many of the early American republics, including the Republic of Vermont, the Republic of West Florida, the State of Franklin, the Cherokee Nation, and the disputed territories of Scotia Maine, Spanish East Florida, the Alabama Range, and the Northwest Indian Lands.

11

The Clarks of Virginia, *soldiers and explorers of distinction*

Virginia-born William Clark who joined Meriwether Lewis on the celebrated overland expedition to the north-west Pacific coast region in 1803 was a second generation Scots-Irishman of a family who moved from Ulster to Pennsylvania and into the Shenandoah Valley in the mid-18th century.

The Clark-Lewis three-year expedition over thousands of miles, through rough mountainous terrain, and during the two extremes of weather, was undertaken at the behest of President Thomas Jefferson and it made a highly significant contribution to America's understanding of that region, as Clark's personal journals of the trek confirmed. His account was published as Original Journals of the Lewis and Clark Expedition 1804-06.

The United States purchased the Louisiana territory in 1803 for 15 million dollars, in a deal completed by Thomas Jefferson. This doubled the country's land size, stretching as it did over 800,000 square miles from the Mississippi River to the Rocky Mountains and Jefferson, still trying to settle still-wild state territories like Kentucky, Tennessee and Mississippi, came on for strong criticism from his political opponents for the Louisiana purchase. To spend 15 million dollars on "a wasteland wilderness was the widest chimera of a moonstruck brain" - howled his critics.

But the President was not deterred and, with the approval of Congress, he ordered Meriwether Lewis to undertake an exploration of the territory. Lewis selected William Clark, an old comrade in arms -

a soldier the Indians called "Red Head" and, right away, they made preparations for what became one of the most momentous journeys in the history of civilised society.

Historians credit the accomplishments of the Lewis-Clark expedition more to the quality of the two commanders than to the general brief laid down by Thomas Jefferson and his Presidential aides. Lewis had a talent for naturalistic observation, while Clark was a skilled map-maker.

The major objectives of the expedition were to explore the Missouri River and determine how easily the American continent could be crossed by this route. Along the way the party would study every aspect of the land - its soil, climate, plant and animal life. Beneath the soil, the explorers would seek out fossil bones and mineral riches. They would offer friendship, trade, education and even vaccination to the Indians, and study every aspect of Indian life - their tribal names, numbers, languages, laws and traditions.

Three boats were used in the expedition, carrying the "Corps of Discovery", 43 people - Lewis, Clark, soldiers, civilians, an Indian interpreter and Clark's black servant York. Starting at Pittsburgh, they descended the Ohio River by keelboat and then ascended the Mississippi to St Louis.

From there they headed up the Missouri River on May 14, 1804, covering 1,400 miles before settling during the first winter with the Mandan Indians in what is now North Dakota and experiencing temperatures as low as 43 degrees below zero, Fahrenheit. In the spring they headed into the Shoshone territory which is now Montana and Indian tribes there provided them with horses for the momentous trek across the Rocky Mountains.

They sighted the Pacific Ocean on November 15, 1805 after passing down the Columbia River. The return journey took most of a year, with the party reaching St Louis in September, 1806. The journey had lasted two years, four months and ten days and they had crossed 7,689 miles of wilderness.

They were the first white men to cross the Continent within the limits of the present-day United States and, incredibly on the perilous journey, only one man lost his life, due to a ruptured appendix - an ailment untreatable in those days even in an eastern hospital.

The main objectives of the expedition were achieved and Clark and Lewis returned with priceless diaries and maps that helped clear up many misconceptions about the north-west territory and bolstered American claims to the region. They also brought back with them animals, plants and minerals which assisted valuable scientific research. They discovered several routes through the Rockies, and established friendly relations with half a dozen Indian tribes. Their topographic sketches showed how people could reach the Pacific Ocean on the overland route via the Rocky Mountains.

The Lewis-Clark expedition may not have been completed without the help of a 16-year-old Shoshoni Indian woman from the Mandan community known as Sacajawea, who was married to a French-Indian trapper and gave birth to a baby just as the party was setting off in the first spring. Sacajawea, carrying her infant son through mountain trails and whitewater streams, guided Lewis and Clark over the Rockies and along the Columbia River to the Pacific.

Sacajawea interpreted for them, rescued their gear when a boat capsized, obtained horses from local Indians and she literally earned herself a place in legend as the Indian princess (her brother was a Shoshoni chief!) who showed America the way west. Lewis and Clark were grateful for her help, but incredibly she was recorded in their journals as "the Indian woman" because they could not spell her name.

William Clark, the youngest of six brothers born to John and Ann Rogers Clark of Charlottesville, Albemarle county, Virginia, moved as a youth to Kentucky with his family and he joined the army in 1789, fighting in the campaign against the Maumee Indians. After the expedition with Lewis, he was appointed brigadier-general in the Louisiana territorial militia and became a US Indian agent in St Louis, before the territory was known as Missouri.

He was the first governor of Missouri in the period 1813-21 and for 16 years was superintendent of Indian affairs, holding responsibility for the welfare of all the trans-Mississippi River tribes. In this role, William Clark was involved in the lucrative western fur trade and, when he died in 1838, aged 68, his funeral was the largest public gathering ever seen in St Louis.

Captain Meriwether Lewis, who was also a Virginian - born in Albemarle county and resident of Charlottesville, was appointed governor of the Louisiana territory in 1806, but in 1809 he died in violent and mysterious circumstances along the Natchez Trace in Middle Tennessee while on his way to Washington. He was only 35 and some historians claim he took his own life because of personal problems and the strains of office.

Near the end of the 1804-06 expedition, Meriwether Lewis wrote in his journal: "The pleasure I felt in having triumphed over the Rocky Mountains and descending once more to a level of fertile country where there was every rational hope of finding a comfortable subsistence for myself and party can be more readily conceived than expressed, nor was the flattering prospect of the final success of the expedition less pleasing."

The Clark-Lewis expedition, which Spain unsuccessfully tried to halt on four counter-expeditions, is widely considered to be the single most impressive and influential feats of exploration in American history.

William Clark's older brother, General George Rogers Clark, was a distinguished Revolutionary War soldier, who in 1778 came to the rescue of Kentucky frontier settlements under attack from British-backed Cherokee Indians. After running the gauntlet of Indian ambushes over 400 miles, Clark managed to get fresh gunpowder supplies to the settlers.

General Clark later led a force of 175 men from Virginia through 180 miles of swamp and forest in Illinois to capture Kastaskia, Cahokia and Vincennes forts. As a result of this intervention, the United States, through the Treaty of Paris, was able to obtain the lands northwest of the Ohio River. Clark's exploits did much to ease the pressures on settlers in the upper Ohio River region.

George Rogers Clark, born at Charlottsville in Virginia, was a surveyor for the Ohio company which traded between Pittsburgh and Kentucky and he later served on the board that supervised allocation of 150,000 acres of land in the Louisville area.

Along with Benjamin Logan, another Scots-Irishman, he also conducted a campaign against the Wabash Indians and Shawnee tribes who were harassing the white settlers in northern Kentucky.

Clark's adventurous militarism in the northwest campaigns after the Revolutionary War was not entirely appreciated by the American establishment and in some ways this made him sympathetically inclined in his later years towards French interests in North America.

In 1793, he wrote to France's US representative Edmund Charles Genet: "My country has proved notoriously ungrateful for my services, but I still have much influence in the West".

In 1793-94 Clark got involved in a plan by the French to capture French Louisiana with the help of 1,500 Kentucky and Tennessee troops and some Indians, but the campaign was aborted when George Washington got wind of it. The President was negotiating a treaty with Spain to open up the Mississippi River and he authorised Kentucky governor Isaac Shelby to halt any movement out of the state.

American author James Alexander Thom, describing the family of George Rogers and William Clark, as heroes, said: "In one generation the Clark family of Virginia fought for our nation's independence, and explored, conquered and settled the continent from sea to shining sea."

Henry Alexander Clark, who was born in Newry, Co Down, is believed to have been a kin of George Rogers and William Clark. He emigrated from Newry in the early part of the 18th century with his parents William Richard and Mary Elizabeth Rogers Clark and the family settled in Virginia.

Clark, who according to his family sources "lived by his wits and his fists and survived", had a close association with George Washington and in 1749 he is recorded as being a chain-carrier for young George, then a surveyor in Virginia. When Washington was made colonel of the Virginia militia, Clark was his orderly sergeant and they made frequent trips across the Blue Ridge Mountains for surveying expeditions and to engage the French and the Indians.

The Clarks were close neighbours of George Washington's parents Augustine and Mary when they lived at Ferry's Farm, Westmoreland county in eastern Virginia. Henry Alexander Clark married English-born Amelia Stafford and they had three sons William, Robert and James, all of whom served in the Revolutionary War under George Washington, in an undercover role.

In 1746 when George Washington was 14, he was apprenticed to survey the lands of Virginia and needing an assistant he chose Henry Alexander Clark, who was a few years older and experienced in the ways of frontier life.

They roamed the foothills of the Blue Ridge Mountains for several years and later, when a 20-year-old Washington was given a commission as major in the Virginia militia, he named Clark as his adjutant, and together they became embroiled in the French-Indian War.

In 1754, Washington received reports about French troops moving from Canada into land west of the Allegheny Mountains, which today would be located in West Virginia. This territory was claimed by both the British and the Virginians, but was still essentially Indian land. The French began to build forts and to befriend the Indians, but Washington took the view that they had no right to settle in the region as families from the Shenandoah Valley had already built homes there.

Robert Dunwiddie, Governor of Virginia, ordered the French off the land and asked Washington to convey this to their commanders. Winter was approaching and the journey was going to be difficult and dangerous, but Washington relished the challenge and invited Henry Alexander Clark to accompany him. They rode horseback over the Blue Ridge Mountains where more supplies were obtained for the trip, and were given pack horses and four men to assist. On the way, they persuaded explorer and Indian trader Christopher Gist to act as their guide.

The group travelled 200 miles to deliver the letter to the French commander and waited several days for a reply. In conversation with French troops and the Indians, it soon became clear to Washington and Clark that the French had no intention of vacating the lands.

Once a negative reply came from the French commander Washington and Clark headed back, encountering bad weather which took them a month to reach the Governor's base at Williamsburg.

It was agreed that Virginians would have to fortify their lands west of the Alleghenies and Washington and Clark were dispatched with company of soldiers to erect the first fort on lands situated on present-day Pittsburgh, Pennsylvania. The fort consisted of huge undressed logs felled in the surrounding forest and General Edward Braddock was called in from England with 1,000 soldiers to defend it.

Washington was one of Braddock's American officers and, both he and Clark warned that fighting conventional English-style was disastrous on the frontier. The French, taking their cue from the Indians, fought from the gullies and behind trees.

Braddock was among those killed in the fighting, but Washington miraculously survived the attacks. It was reported two horses were shot from under him, three bullets went through his hat and one through his clothes, but he was uninjured. Clark was wounded. Washington and he led the Virginian militia in fighting from behind trees and this proved effective.

For his part in defending the fort, Washington was appointed commander of the Virginia forces, with Henry Alexander Clark as his chief aide. The French-Indian war ended with a peace treaty signed in 1763. The pair remained together and when Washington and his wife moved to Mount Vernon in Virginia on the death of his brother Lawrence, Clark became guardian of the estate.

The wound from the French-Indian War and years of exposure on the frontier had weakened Henry Alexander Clark and he was unable to accompany George Washington when he assumed command of the Revolutionary Army. He was assigned to home duties, most notably the army intelligence service which sought to obtain information from behind enemy lines.

Clark's three sons William, Robert and James were also involved in intelligence gathering for the duration of the Revolutionary War, but they never turned up in army records, for security reasons.

They regularly posed as country yokels, in appearance, action and speech; acted dumb and ignorant, but all the time they were fully alert as to what was going on around them. In this undercover work, they were joined by Robert McClellan, another young man of Scots-Irish extraction and whose descendant George Brinton McClellan was a general in the Union Army in the American Civil War. All four played an invaluable role in the Revolutionary War.

Henry Alexander Clark, for his outstanding services in the Revolutionary War, received a land grant in Tennessee, but he was too weak to make the journey by covered wagon and he sent his three sons to settle in Pickett county on the Cumberland Mountain plateau. The settlement was created in an an area known as Clark Mountain and in this virtual wilderness, the Clark family founded a Presbyterian church and a school.

* The Clark connections in the American colonies can be traced back to England, Scotland and the north of Ireland. The Clarks of Upperlands in Co Londonderry stemmed from the 15th century family who were located at Woodchurch in Kent. Later the family

were resident near Abbot's Salford in Warwickshire. St Matthew's Church of Salford Priors is full of arms and memorabilia of Sir Simon Clark (who died in 1651!) and associated families.

About 1680 John Clark, a connection of Simon's, had arrived as a Presbyterian and, probably via Scotland, in the south part of Co Londonderry. A deed survives his purchase of land near Desertmartin in the foothills of the Sperrin Mountains.

By about 1710, John's son Jackson lived at Maghera and was beginning to purchase linen from local weavers, to be bleached and carted to the Dublin markets. Later, Jackson installed the first beetling engine in Co Londonderry, driven by a water wheel on the River Clady in Upperlands. This automated the stamping of linen cloth to impart its prized sheen and smooth texture.

Jackson Clark derived his Christian name from the Jackson family of Coleraine, who were forebears of Thomas Jonathan "Stonewall Jackson, of Civil War fame. There was almost certainly a blood link between the Clarks and the Jacksons, but no marriage in the 17th-18th centuries has yet been traced.

Two children of Jackson Clark, Margaret and Arthur, emigrated and perhaps joined the Thomson family who left Upperlands for Delaware in 1739. Charles Thomson survived orphanage to become, alongside George Washington, a leader of the Independence movement in America and secretary of the First Continental Congress in Philadelphia.

The Rev Dr Adam Clark, the famous preacher born in Maghera, is related through the Clarks of Upperlands to the Virginian Clark family of General George Rogers Clark and his brother William. Another section of the Clark family lived at Grange and Steeple near Antrim town and they too are believed to be linked to the Clarks who settled in the Shenandoah Valley.

The Clarks are still one of the leading families in the South Londonderry area of Northern Ireland, and in Co. Antrim.

* The Rev Dr Thomas Clark, a Presbyterian minister of the Seceder tradition from Ballybay in Co Monaghan, led 300 members of his flock to America in 1764. They sailed from Newry in Co Down and landed at New York. Thomas Clark was well-known as an itinerant minister in counties Armagh, Tyrone, Monaghan and Down.

The Blue Belt: Sacajawea and William Clark on the Upper Missouri River 1805

Shoshoni Indian princess Sacajawea shows Captain William Clark the newly furnished beaded belt she made with blue beads given to her by him and Captain Meriwether Lewis in appreciation of her help in guiding them on their epic expedition to the far west of America.

The significance of the bluebelt is one of friendship and unselfish generosity; of how this courageous young woman gave up one of her most prized possessions to acquire a magnificent sea otter robe that neither Clark nor Lewis had managed to purchase from a Chinook Indian.

The fascinating story of the Blue Belt emerged from the Lewis-Clark "Corps of Discovery" in their remarkable expedition on behalf of President Thomas Jefferson and the American Government from Missouri across the Rocky Mountains to the Pacific Coast in 1804-06.

The Blue Belt painting is by artist David Wright, from Nashville, Tennessee, and is part of the Gray Stone Press (Nashville) collection. We acknowledge courtesy of David Wright and Gray Stone Press for permission to use this and other paintings in the book.

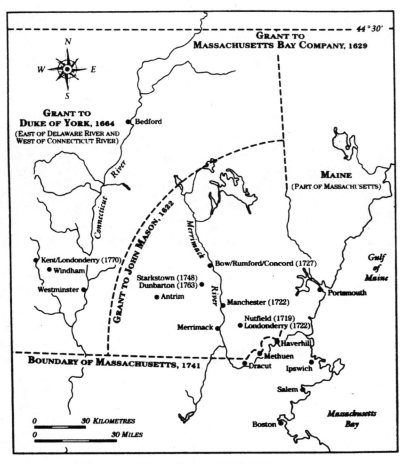

The early Colonial boundaries in New England.

12

Robert Rogers - *leading the charge in the French/Indian War*

Major Robert Rogers, who led the Rogers Rangers in the French-Indian War of 1754-63, was the son of an Ulster Presbyterian couple who moved from Londonderry to America around 1730. As a soldier Rogers used unconventional tactics in warfare, which spawned the concept of light infantry and he later became governor of Michilimackinac (northern Michigan).

His father James Rogers came from Montelony, close to the present-day Northern Ireland town of Dungiven in Co Londonderry, and he married Mary McFatridge several years before they decided to emigrate around 1728. The couple had four children born in Ireland (Daniel, Samuel, Martha and James) and six in America (Robert, Richard, Mary, John, Catherine and Amy).

On arrival in America they lived at Methuen, Massachusetts for several years, an area inhabited by Puritan settlers, but moved north to the Merrimack River territory in 1736 and finally settled in New Hampshire, at Rumford, which is present-day Concord.

New England in the early 18th century was not a particularly welcoming place for Ulster-Scots Presbyterians. The Puritans, whose ancestors had crossed the Atlantic on the Mayflower from Plymouth in England in 1620, eyed them coldly as "a parcel of Irish" and some even damned them as "black Papists." Methuen, however, was a Puritan township which showed some degree of tolerance for the Scots-Irish families who settled there and, with no Presbyterian church in the region, James and Mary Rogers had their children baptised by the local Puritan pastor and attended services regularly.

In Massachusetts, James and Mary Rogers became good friends of Joseph Putney and his family and they acquired land in a nearby region known as the "Great Meadows", with 365 acres allocated to each family. This was a virtual wilderness way off the recognised frontier boundary and, in the spring of 1739, the two families loaded all their possessions on to ox-carts for the movement to the new lands.

James Rogers named his farm Montelony after the townland in the north of Ireland from which they had come and after five years of toil the farms were in a prosperous state, with 100 acres fenced in for haymeadow or animal pasture, with as many more sown to grain, and a sizeable apple orchard. ·

From 1745, the upsurge in violence as a result of French-backed Indian attacks raised serious concerns for families on the outer reaches of the frontier. In May, 1746, the Rogers and Putney families had to make a hasty retreat when scouts arrived to alert them about an Indian war party dispatched by the French from Fort St Frederic on Lake Champlain.

When James Rogers and Joseph Putney returned the next day to retrieve belongings they found the the ruins of their log cabin homes still smouldering, cattle slaughtered and the orchard of apple trees, some already in fruit, destroyed except for one tree

Both families made several attempts to return to their land and rebuild their homes and James Rogers even petitioned the Governor of New Hampshire "praying for assistance against the savages." By 1748, they joined with a group of settlers from Londonderry, New Hampshire, whose families had moved from the Lower Bann Valley region of Ulster in 1718, and formed the township of Starkstown, named after Ulsterman Archibald Stark, along the Massachusetts state line.

Each shareholder in Starkstown received 200 acres, but tragedy struck in 1753 when James Rogers was accidently shot dead by an old hunter friend who mistook him for a bear. It was dusk and folk tradition says Rogers was wearing a bearskin coat.

James Rogers was buried at East Derry, New Hampshire and he left real estate valued at £1,500 and personal property of £444, a considerable amount in those days. Evidently, he prospered when Starkstown was established.

Robert Rogers was born in 1731 when the family lived at Methuen and he grew up in a typical frontier farming community. His soldiering began with the New Hampshire regiment and, after showing exceptional skills as a leader of raids and scouting expeditions in the Merrimack and Contoocook Rivers, he was appointed captain of an independent ranger company, supported by British government funds and consisting of frontiersmen of similar robust stock to Rogers.

This companies were used by the British colonists mainly for reconnaissance against the French and the Indians and in 1758 Rogers was appointed in charge of nine such units. He fought at the battles of Halifax (1757), Ticonderoga (1758) and Crown Point (1759) and in 1760 took part in the final operations against Montreal and then went west to receive the surrender of Detroit and fought engagements from the Scioto River to Sonioto (Shawneetown) on the Ohio River.

Robert Rogers, six feet in stature, always felt the urge to know what was beyond the distant hills. He constantly talked with hunters and Indians about the uncultivated desert, listening and questioning about the mountains, valleys, rivers, lakes and passes. He became not only inured to the hardships faced in the frontier wilderness, but singularly prepared for service in the great beyond.

Robert Rogers, who married Elizabeth Browne, the daughter of Presbyterian clergyman the Rev Arthur Browne, also led an independent company of rangers in operations against the Cherokee Indians in 1761 and he commanded a New York company in the relief and defence of Detroit.

For his brave exploits in soldiering, Rogers received wide acclaim, but his business and financial affairs were not in good shape and he moved to England to escape creditors. During the stay in London in 1765, he published his journals as a hero of the wild and rugged American frontier: Concise Account of North America and Ponteach - The Savages of America, a Tragedy.

In the years leading up to the Revolutionary War, Rogers courted both the American patriots and the British and in 1776 he was imprisoned by General George Washington "as a spy". He strongly denied this charge, declaring: "I love America and I intend to spend the evening of my days in it". He was eventually released.

His political leanings, however, were as a Whig and he escaped to the British and was commissioned to raise the Queen's American Rangers. But this last military charge was shortlived and in 1780 Rogers made it back to England, where he died 15 years later a largely anonymous and impoverished hero.

* Two Londonderry-born brothers James and Hugh Rogers emigrated to America in the Lower Bann Valley Presbyterian exodus of 1718 led by the Rev James MacGregor. They may have earlier family ties back in Ulster, but they are not generally thought to be directly related to James and Mary Rogers.

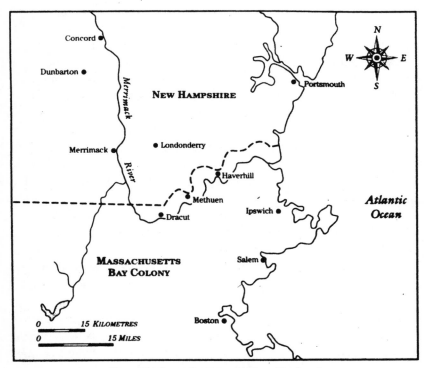

Scots-Irish settlements in New England.

13

Heroes for Christ *on the American frontier*

No American frontier pastor earned the acclaim of his people quite like the Rev Samuel Doak, son of a Co Antrim man who moved to Virginia with other members of his family in the early 1740s. Samuel Doak was a fiery Calvinist preacher and doughty Scots-Irishman who identified totally with his people on the Virginia and Tennessee frontiers. Doak's best-known sermon was delivered to the patriot Overmountain militia men in 1780 before they headed off to the Battle of Kings Mountain, a decisive turning point in the Revolutionary War.

The Overmountain Men, a big percentage of them Scots-Irish, were not soldiers in the real sense, dressed as they were in rough frontier garb and carrying the barest of utensils. But armed with their long rifles and adopting Indian methods of fighting under the shelter of trees and the bushes, they proved more than a match for the Redcoat troops. Samuel Doak, who was just as adept at using a rifle in defence of his kinsfolk and his liberties, was their inspirational chaplain.

Doak's family decided to emigrate after the severe winter of 1739-40 in Ireland - known as "the time of black frost" - which resulted in the deaths of 400,000 people. Drought drove thousands of Ulster Presbyterians to emigrate to America.

Among them were the five Doak brothers (John, Nathaniel, Robert, Daniel, and Samuel) and two sisters (Ann and Thankful). On the journey across the Atlantic, Samuel married one of his kith Jane Mitchell, a widow with three daughters, and they moved through

Pennsylvania to Virginia down the Great Wagon Road, settling on lands at Augusta county.

Their son, the Rev Samuel Doak, was born nine years later and he grew up on the most hazardous frontier existence, working on the family farm until he was 16, acutely aware of the constant dangers from Indian attack.

The Doaks were God-fearing family, who observed all the rituals of their faith, adhering strictly to the teaching of the Bible, catechisms and the Presbyterian Confession of Faith. Samuel was greatly influenced by the piety of his parents and, as a youth, he made his profession of faith and began theological studies for the ministry in Lexington under the Rev Robert Smith, who had emigrated from Londonderry as a young man.

Samuel Doak became a church missionary in south west Virginia, holding a congregational charge at Abingdon, and he also ministered as a circuit rider in the Tennessee territory. When he accepted a call in 1778 from the Hopewell-Concord congregation at Sullivan county in the Watauga settlements along the Holston River area, Doak became the first resident minister to witness in Tennessee.

His church and school house were the first to be erected west of the Allegheny Mountains and his parishioners were like himself the hardiest of the pioneering frontier stock.

In 1780, he moved to Washington county, Tennessee where he formed Salem Presbyterian Church and a school, which was chartered as St Martin's Academy in 1783, later becoming Washington College in 1795. He was College president from 1795 to 1818 before turning it over to his oldest son the Rev John Whitefield Doak.

Surviving the harshness in winter of the East Tennessee mountain environment, attack from hostile Cherokee Indian tribes and the advances of the British colonial forces were the main pre-occupation for these sturdy people and Samuel Doak not only offered pastoral care, but leadership in times of crisis.

In one Cherokee attack while he was away from home, Doak's wife Esther and baby miraculously escaped death. The barking of dogs alerted Esther to the Indian presence and, with the baby asleep in her arms, she quietly escaped into the woods, where she hid.

From her hiding place, she watched the Indians enter the log cabin home, carry out furniture and set fire to the building. The baby did not wake and when the Indians departed she went after dark, by a blind path, to the nearest frontier station and met with her husband the next day.

Samuel Doak's rifle was always at his side, and even when he was in the pulpit preaching the threat of Indian attack was with the settlers daily and very often Doak's sermon was interrupted by a messenger bringing news of a Cherokee attack. Each time, Doak would pray to God for deliverance and if help was needed he would readily join the other men in pursuit of the attackers.

His most momentous hour came on September 25, 1780 at Sycamore Shoals in East Tennessee, where hundreds of Overmountain Men were mustering before heading to Kings Mountain in South Carolina for a battle with British forces.

King George 111 had decreed that the settlers were not to cross the Allegheny Mountains on to what were designated Indian lands, but the edict from London was totally ignored much to the chagrin of the King, who instructed his army officers to retaliate with fire and sword.

Doak, in the vanguard of the American patriot cause, was called upon by Colonel John Sevier to address the militia men and their families. The womenfolk and children had also assembled to bid their farewells and to ensure that the men had enough food and clothing for the assignment on hand.

They too gathered around the pulpit mound as Samuel Doak began his inspirational Old Testament discourse, in which he compared the cause of the Overmountain settlers to that of Gideon and his people in opposing the Midianites in Biblical times.

"The Sword of the Lord and Gideon" he offered up as a battle cry and the fiery sermon and prayer which Samuel Doak delivered that day steeled the Overmountain Men for the march up Gap Creek to the impending confrontation with the British forces, led by King George 111's top soldier Colonel Patrick Ferguson.

Doak's words were characteristic of a frontier cleric in the turbulent years of the late 18th century, but in the two centuries since they have struck a chord with millions of patriotic Americans who hold dear to the liberty secured by the events at Kings Mountain. Samuel Doak did not make it personally to Kings Mountain; he remained at his ministerial charge in the Holston River settlements, continuing the task of winning souls for Christ.

Samuel Doak was a teacher as well as a preacher and, over a period of more than four decades, he founded dozens of churches and schools in the East Tennessee-Virginia-North Carolina region. He actively ministered and taught right up until his death in 1830, aged 81. During the last 12 years of his life, Doak taught at Tusculum College outside Greeneville with his other son the Rev Samuel W. Doak. He is buried at Salem Church in Washington county, Tennessee.

President Theodore Roosevelt, in a tribute to Samuel Doak in his book 'The Winning of the West' wrote: "Possessed of the vigorous energy that marks the true pioneer spirit, he determined to cast in his lot with the frontier folk. He walked through Maryland and Virginia, driving before him an old 'flea-bitten grey' horse, loaded with a sackful of books; crossed the Alleghenies, and came down the blazed trails to the Holston River settlements.

"The hardy people among whom he took up his abode were to appreciate his learning and religion as much as they admired his adventurous and indomitable temper; and the stern, hard, God-fearing man became a most powerful influence for good throughout the whole formative period of the South West".

The Rev John Craig was another Scots-Irish Presbyterian cleric who played a highly significant role in 18th century American frontier life. This Co Antrim-born pastor was the first Presbyterian cleric to minister full-time in the Shenandoah Valley of Virginia and for three decades from 1740 his parish extended for hundreds of miles from his church base at Tinkling Spring in Augusta county.

Craig, described as "a man sent from God to a particular people at a particular time", was a strong advocate of religious liberty and civic freedom and through his influence these essentials of democracy were enshrined in Virginia law.

It was said that the Rev John Craig prepared the seedbed for permanent Presbyterianism in Virginia, from which the church expanded into Tennessee, Kentucky, North Carolina and Georgia.

With a spiritual capacity that was almost inexhaustible, John Craig travelled on horseback to the scattered congregations in the

Shenandoah Valley and in western Virginia. He listed 36 locations where he conferred the sacrament of baptism to hundreds of his flock, both adults and infants.

Like the Rev Samuel Doak, John Craig was an integral part of the Scots-Irish settler community. Outside of his ministerial duties, he farmed and, when necessary, defended his 335-acre homestead at Lewis Creek near Staunton. Craig and his members of his congregations carried long rifles as a precaution against Indian attack.

The Rev Joseph Rhea, one of the first Presbyterian clerics to minister in Tennessee, arrived in America in 1769 as a middle-aged emigrant from Co Donegal and in eight years on the frontier he made a significant contribution to church life. Rhea, of the Campbell clan from lowland Scotland, was born in Londonderry and, after graduation from Glasgow University in 1742, he ministered for 20 years at Fahan and Inch Presbyterian churches in the Innishowen Peninsula in Co Donegal.

Disagreement between the congregation and Joseph Rhea over his annual stipend of £24 led to his resignation and within a month he set sail from Londonderry for Philadelphia with his wife Elizabeth McIlwaine and seven children - John, Matthew, Margaret, William Joseph, Elizabeth and Samuel. Rhea preached for four years at Piney Creek near Taneytown in Maryland, on an annual stipend of £112 (560 dollars), and in 1775 he moved to provide pastoral care in the Holston River settlements in North Carolina which merged to become part of Tennessee.

Joseph Rhea was a scholarly man, a gifted preacher well versed in philosophy, theology and the Hebrew and Latin languages, and he was spoken off as one of the most eminent clerics in Ulster and later on the American frontier.

He fully supported the frontier settlers in their struggle to forge their own identity and democratic structures and acted as chaplain to the patriot troops of Colonel William Christian from the Holston region during a four-week campaign against the Cherokee Indians on the Little Tennessee River.

Rhea was keen to settle his family on lands he bought at Beaver Creek on the Holston River, but when he returned to Maryland in the winter he took pneumonia and died, aged 62. The Rhea family made it to the Tennessee country early in 1778 and subsequent generations left an indelible mark on the community there.

John Rhea, Joseph's eldest son, was a militia soldier, church elder, lawyer, state representative, American Congressman and United States commissioner in treaty talks with the Choctaw Indians. Another son Matthew was a lieutenant in the Virginia Regiment of the Continental Army during the Revolutionary War, while two of his sons fought in the Battle of 1812 with Andrew Jackson.

Matthew Rhea, son of Matthew Sen. and a grandson of the Rev Joseph Rhea, was the first map maker of Tennessee, basing his work on actual land surveys.

The 1832 map of Tennessee incorporated extensive personal observations from Rhea. It clarified the geography of Tennessee and stimulated economic development.

Rhea also accumulated original geologic data on Tennessee and identified an archaeological site that involved the type of aboriginal interment that is now called a stone box burial.

Matthew Rhea later became a teacher at Somerville, Fayette county, Tennessee and his schools attracted pupils from far beyond the state.

14

The Second Great Awakening
on the frontier

In the period after the American Revolutionary War, the frontier settlements were left in a state of chaos, as was most of the country. Lawlessness prevailed and materialism was commonplace. The population of the American "West" or frontier, which by 1800 stretched just beyond the Mississippi River, grew rapidly.

In 1770, Georgia, Tennessee, Kentucky and Ohio had combined populations of about 30,000 souls. By 1810, more than 1,200,000 lived in these states.

Organised religion generally reacts slowly to change of any kind, including mass migration and population growth. The leadership of the Presbyterian Church tried to adhere to old rules and ways that worked well in the eastern seaboard regions, but were difficult to apply in places like East Tennessee and Kentucky.

There were just a few volunteers from the Scots-Irish community ministering for God in the south eastern Appalachians during the latter part of the 18th century and it is remarkable what was achieved in terms of church planting there.

The Rev Charles Cummings, a native of Ulster, laboured along the Holston River in southern Virginia for three decades beginning in 1773 and preached in present-day Sullivan and Hawkins counties in Tennessee shortly after the Revolution. The Rev Samuel Doak, a Princeton graduate, arrived in Tennessee in 1778, preaching with a rifle at his side and one ear cocked for warnings of marauding Indians. The Rev David Rice visited Kentucky in 1783 and returned to settle a large family, thus earning the title - "Father of Western Presbyterianism."

These three were typical of the few clergymen ministering to a land-grabbing, war-worn people, a large proportion of whom were undereducated and irreligious. The odds were not good. Something had to change.

Around 1790, there began a religious awakening movement that became known as the Second Great Awakening. Most historians say the movement started on the campus of Hampden Sidney College in Virginia. However, there had been winds of change in the Piedmont region of North Carolina in the same period. These changes took the form of divisions in existing congregations. Some worshippers at services began to exhibit physical manifestations of their faith, crying out to God, shouting "Amen" whenever the spirit moved them, and swaying as they sang hymns. Lines were drawn between those who believed this behaviour proper and those who did not.

The Rev James McGready, one of the best known of the early itinerant preachers, was born in Pennsylvania, but was a resident of Guilford county in North Carolina by 1778. He joined Buffalo Presbyterian Church at the age of 17 and he was in Kentucky and upper Tennessee preaching a "modified form of Calvinism" - by 1797.

By 1801, revivalism had a foothold in the Overhill settlements and at a camp meeting in at Cane Ridge, Kentucky around 25,000 people gathered to be baptised and to rise again as God's people. Ministers of several denominations were on hand and two of them are believed to have been the Rev James McGready and the Rev Benjamin Lakin, a grand old Methodist-Episcopal preacher.

These men had brought a more free-wheeling, fundamentalist form of religion to the upper Cumberland River region and one of the families it struck a chord with was the McDonnolds, who moved from Co Antrim to America in the mid-18th century and were in East Tennessee by 1785.

The McDonnold family gradually moved west to upper Middle Tennessee as former Indian lands were opened up for settlement. At the time of arrival in America, the family consisted of a widowed mother (Judith), four sons and a daughter, all intent on making good in their new surroundings. Members of the family were to become surveyors, lawyers, doctors and judges.

By 1810, when the Second Great Awakening, was in full bloom, the McDonnolds were a largely extended clan, who had developed strong and lasting associations with people of similar religious and political leanings, and, in time, the family were part of the Cumberland Presbyterian Church.

This "indigenously Southern" denomination exists today with about 100,000 members and, though the origins of Cumberland Presbyterianism are somewhat misunderstood, its beginnings can be explained in the words of the hymn - "Here Am I Lord . . . I will go, Lord . . !" The Cumberland Presbyterians did not originally set out to start a new religion. However the founding pastors - Samuel King, Finnis Ewing, and Samuel McAdow - realised that on basic issues of faith and interpretation of the scriptures they were separated from their Eastern brethren.

They were ministering among settlers who had gone to war over the right of self-determination and to paraphrase the words of King, Ewing and McAdow: "There are no eternal reprobates; Christ died for all, not for a few, children dying in infancy are saved through Christ and because they have not elected to sin; the Spirit of God operates on the word - in such a manner as to leave all men inexcusable".

The first McDonnolds to become pastors in the Cumberland Presbyterian movement were James and Philip, sons of Redmond, grandsons of Judith. Philip as a young man was a highly charismatic individual, who was described as a great orator, with the ability to engage and hold a congregation. He headed off into the forests to prepare his sermons and it was said his message was delivered with every ounce of strength he possessed, to the extent that he was often emotionally and physically drained by his work.

The elders of the Cumberland Presbyterian Church were drawn by Philip's devotion and his ability to lead souls to Christ. They contributed to his higher education and he rewarded their trust with total commitment. Philip married in 1814 Mary Baker Ewing, the niece of one of the Cumberland Presbyterian Church's fathers - the Rev Finnis Ewing, but a year later he died, leaving his son Philip Monroe McDonnold to follow in his footsteps as a Cumberland Presbyterian minister.

According to a published obituary, the Rev James McDonnold was born in 1790 in Greene county, Tennessee. His mother's name is not known although it is believed she died while giving birth and the boys were raised by their father, with ample assistance from their Ulster-born grandmother Judith.

James McDonnold's path to the ministry was not an easy one. He was a surveyor by profession and did militia duties and when he made a decision to become a minister, he was told by the Cumberland Presbyterian leadership to go home and study grammar and other required subjects. He was ordained in 1816, the year after his brother Philip's death, and he and his wife Margaret Grier had four children.

James continued to work as a surveyor since in those days ministers received no compensation for their services unless a settler offered a few ears of corn or a warm meal. His first circuit was among the trappers, traders and Indians who then occupied what is now West Tennessee and, later, he founded Cave Spring Church near Livingston in Overton county, Tennessee.

James was a hardworking individual whose greatest asset as a minister was probably his physical endurance, commitment to education and an understanding of his fellow man.

In 1838, James was sent by the Cumberland Presbyterian Church to form a second presbytery, in the war-torn Republic of Texas. Life was difficult for Protestant church missionaries in early Texas. Non-believers taunted them when they preached and very often they were run out of town. In September, 1838, shortly after his arrival in Texas, the Rev James McDonnold and his fellow Cumberland Presbyterian ministers were forced to move their regular meeting in the Gossett community on the Trinity River because the location was broken up by Indians.

A few weeks before his death from malaria in 1853, James McDonnold addressed his fellow ministers, with a message about bringing the Good News and schooling to the widows and orphans of his adopted Lone Star State, despite their inability to contribute financially to the Church.

Among the members of the Cave Spring Church was Thomas K. McDonnold, who was known as "Doubting Thomas" because he often resisted many attempts to save his soul. Finally, the elders of the Church elected to let Thomas K. find his own way and it was said that through this method his conversion came about. Thomas, son of John

McDonnold, a brother of Redmond, was the father of the Rev Benjamin Wilburn McDonnold, who was President of Tennessee's Cumberland University in the years after the American Civil War. Religion and education were in a state of upheaval in the South at the time and Benjamin McDonnold's teaching ministry helped stabilise the situation.

Benjamin had previously been a professor of mathematics, and a chaplain in the Confederate Army. He died in 1889, aged 62, after writing a monumental work titled, History of the Cumberland Presbyterian Church.

* Up to 20 direct descendants of the original McDonnold immigrants or who married into the family were ministers of the Cumberland Presbyterian Church, Presbyterian Church USA or the Church of Christ.

The Rev. George Whitefield.
Though the actual founder of Methodism, George Whitefield yielded leadership of the movement to John Wesley in order to devote his full attention to evangelism in both England and the Americas. His brilliant oratory and simple gospel theme made him an influential figure on both sides of the Atlantic. He was a primary human agency behind the Great Awakening in America.

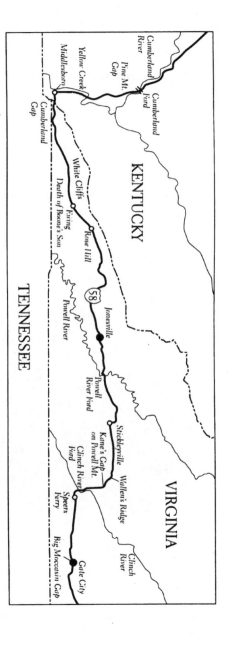

Daniel Boone's Wilderness Road from Big Mocassin Gap in Virginia to Cumberland Ford in Kentucky.

15

Benjamin Logan - *pioneer who set up ordered structures in Kentucky*

Next to Daniel Boone, Benjamin Logan was the leading pioneer soldier and politician in the settlement of Kentucky during the late 18th century and in very difficult days in the "dark and bloody land" Logan's distinctive Scots-Irish characteristics of courage and dogged determination stood out.

Logan was born at Augusta county in the Shenandoah Valley of Virginia, the son of an Ulster-born couple David and Jane (McKinley) Logan, who had moved from the north of Ireland in the early 1740s. He and his younger brother John were baptised at the New Providence Church by the Rev John Craig, from Co Antrim who was the first Presbyterian minister in the Shenandoah Valley.

Their father David and uncle James served as members of the Virginia militia in the French-Indian Wars of 1754-63 and Benjamin was a militia recruit at 16. He inherited his father's estate in 1757, but instead of taking it for himself, sold it and divided the proceeds among the other members of the family. This led to further land speculations which made Benjamin one of the wealthiest men in the region.

Benjamin moved to the Holston River area of south-western Virginia, marrying Ann Montgomery and settling at Black's Station, site of the present-day town of Abingdon near the Tennessee state border. There he was closely involved with Colonel John Donelson, leader of the Watauga movement, and James Knox, a surveyor and a hunter widely acknowledged as "leader of the Long Hunters".

He participated in the Governor Dunmore war campaign against Indian tribes in 1774 which opened up the Kentucky lands to white settlers and, within a year had set up a frontier stockade at St Asaph in eastern Kentucky. He became the first sheriff of Kentucky county and in 1781 led militia attacks on Shawnee Indian tribes along the Ohio River.

His experience as a Republican legislator on the Virginia assembly equipped Logan for service on the various conventions which resulted in the establishment of Kentucky as a state in 1792 and the first Governor Isaac Shelby appointed him major general in the state militia, with a full division of soldiers under his command.

In 1796, Logan along with three others sought the nomination to succeed Governor Isaac Shelby, but, although a highly popular figure in the Kentucky frontier communities, he was just pipped for the post by a fellow Republican James Garrard.

Logan's leadership of the essentially Scots-Irish community in the early formative years of the new settlements of Kentucky was totally practical and meaningful. Like his kinsfolk, he worked from dawn to dusk, both in farming the lands and providing defence against hostile Indian attacks.

St Asaph's stockade was highly vulnerable to Cherokee Indian attack and defences had to be maintained at all times. In one attack on May 23, 1777, the fort was besieged by a force of 100 Indians and the womenfolk weighed in behind the men in resisting the attack. Frontier women needed to be handy with a rifle when danger presented itself.

There were fatalities in this attack, including William Hudson, who was struck down while out rounding up the livestock. Burr Harrison, another close associate of Logan, was injured and died later from his wounds and most of the livestock was targeted, a favoured ploy by the Indians.

Another attack was imminent and with food supplies and gun powder low, Logan left the fort for the Holston settlements in western Virginia to seek reinforcements. A second Indian attack came in late August, but before the reinforcements reached the fort, Ambrose Grayson, one of Logan's men, was killed and two companions wounded as they ventured out for corn supplies.

On Grayson's body, the Indians left several copies of a British proclamation, signed by a Colonel Henry Hamilton, which detailed instructions from London about deploying Indians against the white settlers, mostly of Scots-Irish origin, who were in revolt against the Crown in the Revolutionary War. The proclamation offered food, lodging and humane treatment to all who deserted the American cause and presented themselves to any British post.

Those who would take up arms against the Americans and continue "until the extinction of the rebellion" were promised "pay adequate to their former stations in the rebel service". All common men who "shall serve during that period shall receive His Majesty's bounty of 200 acres of land".

When Benjamin Logan was shown copies of the proclamation, he realised their implications for the morale of his men and he quietly hid them. The British had forged an alliance with the Indians and a bid was made to buy off wavering white settlers, but it did not work.

For several decades, St Asaph's or Logan's fort was a dangerous outpost on the Kentucky frontier and it needed raw courage from Benjamin Logan and the brave clutch of men and womenfolk who surrounded him. Logan and his wife Ann had nine children, five sons and four daughters, and Benjamin died in 1802, after spending the last years of his life in constitutional politics.

John Logan, Benjamin's brother, was also a militia officer and was the first state treasurer of Kentucky for five years from 1792. John had been on various expeditions against the Indians, was a Virginia legislator and was involved in the Kentucky statehood conventions. He married Jane McClure and they had six daughters and a son.

In 1795, John Logan, acting on authority from Kentucky Governor Isaac Shelby, joined James Knox and Daniel Boone in hiring surveyors and road cutters at a wage of two shillings and sixpence daily to improve the Wilderness Road route through the Cumberland Gap for the many migrant families trekking into the region from eastern states.

The McAfee family were Scots-Irish associates in Kentucky of the Logans, with Robert Breckinridge McAfee, a leading state legislator of the early 19th century, the grandson of Ulster pioneers James and Jane McAfee, who emigrated to Pennsylvania about 1740.

The couple's three sons - Robert, James Jun. and George - and son-in-law James McCoun set up McAfee's station in Mercer county, Kentucky. Robert McAfee was known as the "First Commodore of Western Rivers" for his operation of the first flatboats to New Orleans via the Ohio and Mississippi Rivers. Robert was murdered at New Orleans during one of these expeditions.

His son Robert Brackinridge McAfee became a guardian on the death of his parents to John Brackinridge, the attorney general of the United States in the cabinet of President Thomas Jefferson. He was elected to the Kentucky state legislature and senate from Mercer county; was the state's first lieutenant governor and was an influential figure in Andrew Jackson's Democratic Party.

He served for five years as charge d'affaires to the republic of Columbia in South America and he fought under Andrew Jackson in the War of 1812.

The three McAfee brothers founded the New Providence Presbyterian Church at Mercer county, naming it for what they saw as the work of God's providence during dark and dangerous days in Kentucky. New Providence was one of the first churches established in the territory.

Badge of Kentucky.

16

The distinguished line *of Fighting Jacks*

Three American Presidential First Ladies are all reputed to be directly related to Revolutionary War hero Captain James Jack, whose father Patrick emigrated to Pennsylvania in 1762 from a farm at Ardstraw in the Sperrin mountain region of Co Tyrone.

Mary Todd, wife of President Abraham Lincoln; Edith Carow, second wife of President Theodore Roosevelt and Helen "Nellie" Herron, wife of President William Howard Taft, have ancestral ties to Captain Jack, one of the principal signatories of the Mecklenburg Declaration in North Carolina on May 20, 1775 which was the forerunner of the Declaration of Independence on July 4, 1776.

The Jacks (Jacques) were originally French Huguenot Protestants who because of religious persecution in the 17th century had to flee to Scotland, and subsequently to the north of Ireland. The family were Presbyterians in Scotland and Ulster and they took their Calvinist faith to America.

Patrick Jack settled at Chambersburg, Pennsylvania before moving to Charlotte in North Carolina, a region referred to by British commander Lord Charles Cornwallis as the "Hornet's Nest" because of its commitment to the American revolutionary cause.

There, Patrick Jack and his five sons were active participants in the Revolutionary War and were continually on a wanted list by British troops. The family home at Charlotte was burned by forces led by the despised Redcoat officer Banastre Tarleton after Patrick Jack was taken by his family and hid in a surrounding forest.

James Jack, a nephew of Patrick, was killed in the Revolutionary War and his 17-year-old son James took his place in the battle lines. James and Jeremiah Jack are listed as revolutionary patriots of the Battle of Kings Mountain in October 1780.

Mrs Helen Taft, the daughter of Judge John Williamson Herron, of Cincinnati, Ohio, came through this side of the family. Judge Herron's family are also related to the Rev Dr Francis Herron, minister of First Pittsburgh Presbyterian Church in Pennsylvania from 1811 to 1861. The Rev Herron's father came from Rathfriland in Co Down.

The Jack family supplied the only cleric to be named twice as Moderator of the Presbyterian Church of the United States - the Rev Samuel Jack Nicholl, who, for 50 years, was pastor of the Fourth Presbyterian Church at St Louis, Missouri. Another of the Jack clan was George Shiras Jun., who was a distinguished Justice of the Supreme Court of the United States.

The Jacks were a pioneering family in the move west and south during the late 18th century and the early part of the 19th century and one illustrious kinsman Colonel William Houston Jack joined Colonel Jim Bowie in leading 140 infantry and cavalry soldiers of the Texan Revolutionary Army against 150 men from the Republic of Mexico Army in the Grass Fight at San Antonio, Texas in November, 1835.

This battle, which resulted in a minor victory for the Texans, was a prelude to the siege of The Alamo in March, 1836, where Jim Bowie and Davy Crockett and Texas Rangers and Tennessee compatriots perished at the hands of Mexican insurgents, and the Battle of San Jacinto in April of that year, which resulted in a famous victory for General Sam Houston and his men over the Mexicans in his "Save Texas" campaign.

The Grass Fight was so named when the Texans found freshly cut grass found in the mule packs left by the fleeing Mexican soldiers instead of silver bullion which was rumoured to be on its way to San Antonio. One consolation for the Texans was that they were able to recover animals and equipment worth 2,000 dollars which they later auctioned. Four of their men were wounded and one deserted and fifteen Mexicans were counted dead on the field, but Jim Bowie reckoned enemy casualties were as high as sixty.

William Houston Jack, a Georgian who moved to Texas from Alabama in 1832, was a lawyer and a member of the constitutional committee agitating for Texas independence.

A John Jack is recorded as being a Scots-Irish settler of Chester county, Pennsylvania and Frederick county, Maryland in the period 1734-54.

* Mecklenburg county, bordering on the Waxhaws region where President Andrew Jackson was born, was a Scots-Irish stronghold where the family of another President of Ulster vintage James Knox Polk were leading citizens.

Mary Todd Lincoln, wife of President Abraham Lincoln.

Helen Herron Taft, wife of President William Howard Taft.

Historic landmark
on the frontier

John Harris MD,
Greenville Presbyterian Church,
South Carolina
First minister 1773-1784, a patriot of the
American Revolution.

*"Sacred to the memory of the Scots-Irish
pioneers who organised this Presbyterian
Church AD 1784. From the home land they
brought their faith to enrich the South. Their
brave hearts and strong arms to subdue the
wilderness".*

In Memorium

JANE WILSON
Secretary of the Donalds Historical Society, South Carolina.
Died tragically on March 17, 2000.

•••

*Jane was deeply committed to the preservation and promotion
of Scots-Irish history and culture in the United States and
she contributed much to the Scots-Irish Chronicles.*

17

Christopher "Kit" Carson - *daring mountain man of the American West*

Christopher 'Kit' Carson, a Kentuckian of a Scots-Irish family who had moved from Ulster to America in the mid-18th century, was an Indian fighter, scout and frontiersman who explored the far west and the south into Mexican territory for upwards of 50 years.

Carson was born at Madison county, Kentucky where his family were close associates of Daniel Boone and Kit grew up in Missouri. He gained an apprenticeship as a saddle-maker and, after leaving home at the age of 17, teamed up with a band of traders moving in the direction of the Rocky Mountains.

For most of a decade, Carson was involved in the lucrative business of beaver trapping and he was also a driver on the wagon trains hauling freight across the Santa Fe Trail which opened up in the 1820s. Carson guided a US-government funded expedition to California in 1842-46 and in 1842 assisted the noted Western explorer John Charles Fremont in making an accurate map of the Oregon Trail, which detailed such things as campsites and estimates of possible daily travel.

"Kit" Carson was also a guide to the force that captured California during the Mexican War and in 1853 he became the Indian agent at Taos, New Mexico.

During the Gold Rush of 1849 Carson was involved in the delivery of half a million sheep from New Mexico to California. The gold miners were prepared to pay a good price for the sheep.

When the Civil War began, Carson joined the Union Army, serving as a colonel in the New Mexico Volunteers, and for a short time he commanded Fort Union, the US army's largest post at the strategic point of the mountain branch and the Cimarron Cutoff of the Santa Fe Trail.

Carson, a small stooped-shouldered man with red hair and freckled face, made a number of successful forays against the warring Mescalero Apache and Navajo Indian tribes. In January, 1868, he was appointed superintendent of Indian affairs for the Colorado territory, but died in May of that year aged only 58.

Despite his diminutive stature, Christopher 'Kit' Carson was a man of extraordinary courage and daring and his activities were legendary in the rapid expansion of American interests on the southern and western frontiers during the mid-19th century.

Tradition states that once the colourful Carson and a lone companion took on and defeated 30 outlaw Indians. For a century and a half, dozens of books and comic strips have covered his remarkable wild frontier exploits.

Robert Campbell was another Scots-Irishman who distinguished himself as a frontier mountain man in the 19th century America. Born in the north of Ireland in 1804 of Scots ancestry, he emigrated when he was 18 and eventually made it to the Rocky Mountains where he became involved in fur trading.

Campbell took part in the 1832 battle of Pierre's Hole which involved the mountain men and several hundred Indians of the Blackfeet tribe. During the Mexican War he raised and drilled a regiment of Missouri volunteers and progressed as a successful St Louis businessman. He died in 1879.

18

Ulysses S. Grant - *brave farmer's son who was superior as a General*

U lysses Simpson Grant, who heroically led the Union Army to victory in the American Civil War and was the 18th United States President, is of Co Tyrone farming stock. His great-grandfather on his mother Hannah's side John Simpson left Ulster for Pennsylvania in 1760 and after passing through the Shenandoah Valley of Virginia the Simpson family eventually settled in Ohio.

The Simpson family homestead at Dergenagh is situated about five miles west of the town of Dungannon in Co Tyrone. The family was Presbyterian, although Ulysses Grant was a nominal Methodist, who, although he did not attend church regularly, spoke often about his belief in God, the Bible and an afterlife.

On his father's side, Grant's original immigrant forebear Matthew Grant emigrated from Plymouth, England to Dorchester, Massachusetts in 1630 shortly after the movement of the Pilgrim Fathers. His great-grandfather Captain Noah Grant was killed in action in 1756 during the French-Indian War and his grandfather, also Captain Noah Grant, served on the revolutionary side during the War of Independence, and he fought at Bunker Hill.

Ulysses, the rugged soldier-politician was born on a farm at Mount Pleasant, Ohio in 1822 and, after he graduated from West Point military college in 1843 standing 21st in a class of 39, he was involved as a captain in army assignments in Missouri, Louisiana and Mexico, where he earned a citation for bravery.

After the Mexican War, Grant resigned his commission in 1854 because of loneliness, depression and a desperate need to be with his wife Julia and young family. Julia was a tower of strength to Grant when he was in depressive moods, very often brought on by an over-indulgence in alcohol, and it was her steadying influence that pushed him to the pinnacles of his military and political careers.

By the start of the Civil War in 1861, Grant returned to service and he was a colonel in the Illinois volunteer infantry regiment of the Union Army. Within a short time he graduated to brigadier general. His leadership was evident in the Kentucky-Tennessee campaign of 1862, which led to the capturing of Fort Henry and Fort Donelson from the Confederates. Raised on a farm, Grant had a great love of horses and he seemed to be always at his best on horseback.

At Shiloh in April of that year, his regiment sustained a lot of casualties, but they recovered and eventually overcame the Confederates. Grant's unconventional tactics in the field and his uncharacteristic manner and shabby appearance for a senior officer brought criticism, but Abraham Lincoln rejected calls for his dismissal, stating: "I can't spare this man. He fights".

Lincoln's belief in Grant, untutored and a shy retiring man of changing moods, paid off. With systematic authority and unflinching calculation, he skilfully turned things around for the Northern forces, with significant successes at Vicksburg on the Mississippi River and at Chattanooga in Tennessee. In March, 1864 Lincoln appointed him his commander-in-chief.

The War was in its final phase with the Confederates losing out in men and resources and Grant moved on Virginia where General Robert E. Lee was based, while his successor in Tennessee General W. T. Sherman marched into Georgia towards Atlanta.

The summer of 1864 saw Grant and Lee engaging in some of the most bloody battles of the War at The Wilderness, Spotsylvania, Cold Harbour and Petersburg, with tens of thousands of men lost on both sides. The most decisive battle for Grant came in the spring of 1865 when, backed up by General Philip Sheridan, he managed to outflank Lee's Confederate troops in the Shenandoah Valley.

Grant offered Lee generous terms of surrender, with the assurance that Confederate soldiers would be paroled and allowed home to their various southern states. Lee signed the surrender document at Appomattox Court House on April 9 and, over the summer, General Grant supervised the dismantling of the Union Army.

In a tribute to Grant, General Robert E. Lee said: "I have carefully searched the military records of both ancient and modern history and have never found Grant's superior as a general".

President William McKinley said of Grant: "Faithful and fearless as a volunteer soldier, intrepid and invincible as commander-in-chief of the armies of the Union and confident as President of a reunited and strengthened nation, which his genius has been instrumental in achieving".

After the War, Grant was nominated for Secretary of State by President Andrew Johnson, but he was never approved for that office by Congress. He did, however, make it to the President in 1868 after accepting the Republican nomination.

Grant's reputation as a victorious war general made him a popular figure in the North and, without much electioneering, and a simple poll theme - "let us have peace", he won an overwhelming mandate, defeating New York Democrat Horatio Seymour. In his inaugural Presidential address, he said: "I ask patient forbearance one toward another throughout the land, a determined effort on the part of every citizen to do his share toward cementing a happy Union". In 1872, his Presidential success over another New Yorker Horace Greeley was even more convincing.

Grant, however, fully realised his shortcomings as a politician and he has never enjoyed high rating as an American President. At the end of his two terms in the White House he said: "It was my fortune, or misfortune, to be called to the office of Chief Executive without any previous political training".

And on his army career, he modestly commented: "The truth is I am more of a farmer than a soldier. I never went into the army without regret and never retired without pleasure". His military prowess spoke for itself and in war he operated with the simple formula: find the enemy, hit them hard and move on.

The American Civil War was very costly for both sides in terms of lives lost, but it is widely acknowledged that Grant's triumphs were down to his commonsensical approach to generalship, emphasis on co-ordination and co-operation, calmness under pressure, determination to achieve his goals, energy in action and a resourcefulness, perseverance and decisiveness in the heat of battle.

Ulysses Simpson Grant died in July, 1885 after suffering from a painful throat cancer. An estimated million people turned out for his funeral in New York.

* In 1878, Ulysses S. Grant was made a freeman of Londonderry, today Northern Ireland's second city and from where many Scots-Irish immigrants left for America in the 18th century.

The honour recognised both Grant's gallantry as a soldier and his service as an American statesman, not forgetting his 18th century Ulster roots.

In July, 1878, Grant travelled to Ireland as part of a world tour to receive the Londonderry freemanship, arriving in Dublin and travelling by train to Londonderry via Omagh and Strabane. He stopped off for a period at Ballygawley in Co Tyrone to see the Grant family homestead and before he moved on he also stopped off at Coleraine.

During his stay in Londonderry, President Grant, who was accompanied by a number of American friends and aides, was keenly interested in hearing the full story of the famous Siege in the city in 1688-89 and he was given a full tour of the famous walls of Derry, remarking on their thickness.

THE INAUGURAL ADDRESS OF PRESIDENT ULYSSES S. GRANT ON MARCH 4, 1869: "The country having just emerged from a great rebellion, many questions will come before it for settlement in the next four years which preceding Administrations have never had to deal with. In meeting these it is desirable that they should be approached calmly, without prejudice, hate, or sectional pride, remembering that the greatest good to the greatest number is the object to be attained. This requires security of persons, property, and free religious and political opinion in every part of our common country, without regard to local prejudice. All laws to secure these ends will receive my best efforts for their enforcement."

President Andrew Jackson and his wife Rachel.

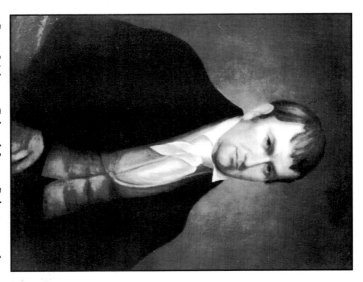

Scots-Irishman Colonel James Robertson, who along with Colonel John Donelson in 1780 founded Fort Nashborough, which became the city of Nashville.

The memorial in Nashville to the city's founder, Colonel James Robertson.

David Crockett, Tennessee frontiersman-politician and hero of the siege of The Alamo. (John Gadsby Chapman's oil portrait and Chester Harding's picture of Crockett in 1834).

The Alamo in San Antonio, where 189 men were killed in March 1836, fighting for the independence of Texas. Nine of those killed were Irish-born and many others belonged to Scots-Irish families from Tennessee, Virginia, North Carolina and Kentucky.

*Sam Houston, Governor of Tennessee and Texas, and the man who
commanded the routing of the Mexican army at the battle of San Jacinto
after the siege of The Alamo. Houston's family were Presbyterian stock from
Co. Antrim, emigrating to the Shenandoah Valley of Virginia in the mid-18th
century. (Portrait in oils by Boris B. Gordon 1935).*

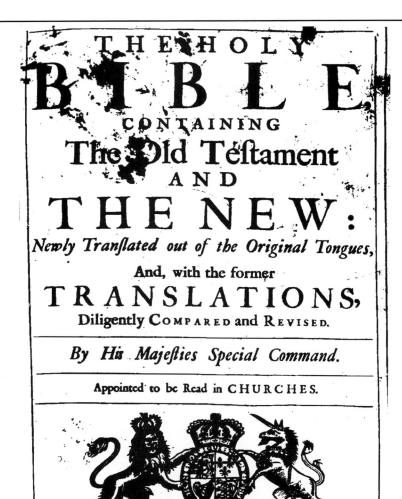

THE HOLY
BIBLE
CONTAINING
The Old Testament
AND
THE NEW:
Newly Tranflated out of the Original Tongues,
And, with the former
TRANSLATIONS,
Diligently COMPARED and REVISED.

By Hü Majefties Special Command.

Appointed to be Read in CHURCHES.

DUBLIN:
Printed by A. RHAMES; for ELIPHAL DOBSON, at the *Stationers-Arms* in *Caftle-ftreet*, and WILLIAM BINAULD, at the *Bible* in *Euftace-ftreet*, MDCCXIV.

Opening page of the Dublin-printed Bible belonging to William Irvine
Lewis, who died at The Alamo, Texas in March 1836. Lewis, a Virginian,
was descended from a Scots-Irish Presbyterian family from Ulster who
settled in the Shenandoah Valley.

General Thomas Jonathan 'Stonewall' Jackson, Confederate officer in the American Civil War. His great-grandfather John Jackson was born in Ulster.

James Ewell Brown Stuart, a Confederate general in the Civil War whose great-great-grandfather came from Londonderry.

Ulysses S. Grant, commander of the Union Army in the American Civil War, and United States President over two terms in 1869-77. Grant's great grandfather, John Simpson, left Dergenagh outside Dungannon, Co. Tyrone for America in 1760.

The fur trapper in the Rocky Mountains during the early part of the 19th century. One of the most famous trappers was Christopher 'Kit' Carson (inset), whose Scots-Irish settler family had set up home in Kentucky. (Painting - David Wright, Nashville).

The 1804-06 Western expedition through the Rocky Mountains to the Pacific region by William Clark and Meriwether Lewis. Clark's family had direct links back to Ulster. (Painting - David Wright, Nashville).

The Long Knife painting by Nashville artist David Wright depicts a typical American frontiersman of the 18th century.

Charles Thomson, born in Maghera, Co. Londonderry, who was Secretary to the Continental Congress of America for 15 years after the Revolutionary War and designer of the Great Seal of America.

General George Rogers Clark, Scots-Irish Virginia militia man and Kentucky pioneer.

*President Woodrow Wilson, whose grandfather James Wilson
emigrated from Strabane, Co. Tyrone to America in 1807.*

General Benjamin Logan, 18th century Kentucky pioneer, son of Ulster-born parents.

The Rev. Samuel Doak, 18th century Virginia and Tennessee frontier Presbyterian pastor and son of a Co. Antrim-born couple who emigrated to America in 1740.

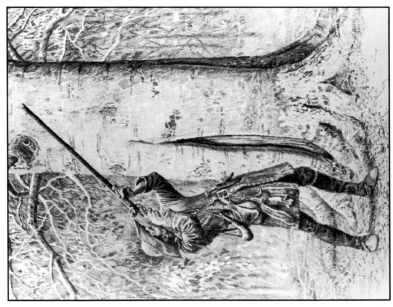

A typical American frontiersman, always on the alert. Shooting at squirrels! (Paintings by David Wright, Nashville).

Crossroads to Destiny - October 1813! Four men of the hour meet up at Camp Blount, Lincoln County, Tennessee. General Andrew Jackson (on horseback); Ensign Sam Houston of the 39th US Infantry Regiment; David Crockett, of the 2nd Regiment Volunteer Mounted Riflemen and Dr. Charles McKinney, from Fayetteville, Tennessee, who accompanied General Jackson's Army during the War of 1812-14. All four were of Scots-Irish family roots.
(Painting by David Wright, Nashville).

19

The special qualities of
Thomas Jonathan "Stonewall" Jackson

Thomas Jonathan "Stonewall" Jackson figures high in the list of Scots-Irish heroes whose outstanding courage and military prowess gave him an honoured place in the annals of American history. "Stonewall" Jackson may have fought and died on the losing Confederate side during the Civil War of 1861-65, but he was a soldier of special quality and his upright Christian ideals marked him down as a true leader of men.

Jackson was given the nickname "Stonewall" at the Battle of Bull Run in Virginia in July, 1861 after it was said of him: "This is Jackson, standing a stone wall". The highly significant role that he played for the Confederates in this decisive battle earned him promotion to Major General.

The Civil War hero was the great grandson of an Ulsterman John Jackson, who at the age of 33 emigrated to America in 1748 as "a respectable and prosperous tradesman", settling first in Maryland, and then putting down his roots in the Shenandoah Valley of Virginia after passing through West Virginia.

John Jackson's family were lowland Presbyterian Scots who settled in the north of Ireland during the 17th century Scottish Plantation years and defended Londonderry during the Siege of 1688-89. The Jacksons were scattered across Ulster, some located in the north west of the Province, around Londonderry and Coleraine, while others lived in counties Armagh, Down and Antrim.

Varying claims are made about exactly where in Ulster John Jackson was born. In the biography of "Stonewall" Jackson by

English writer Lieutenant Colonel G. F. R. Henderson a letter is referred to which states that the ancestors of the great Confederate general had lived in the parish of Londonderry.

This letter, according to Henderson, was in the possession of Thomas Jackson Arnold, of Beverly, West Virginia , a nephew of General Jackson. Another report, of American origin, gives John Jackson's birthplace as near Coleraine in Co Londonderry.

Local residents, however, in the Birches-Tartaraghan area of Co Armagh close to the shores of Lough Neagh in the centre of Ulster are adamant that John Jackson was one of their kin. Their belief is borne out by a plaque unveiled on July 22, 1967 in Ballinary, a section of the Birches, which states that this was the reputed birthplace of John Jackson, great grandfather of Thomas Jonathan "Stonewall" Jackson (1824-1863). The then United States Consul-General in Northern Ireland unveiled the plaque at the Ballinary site, which is located some 70 miles from Londonderry-Coleraine.

Today, there are reportedly more Jacksons living in this part of Co Armagh than in any other region of Northern Ireland and they are convinced of the local connection with "Stonewall" Jackson's family. John Jackson is traced by the Co Armagh Jacksons to be a grandson of Robert Jackson and a son of John Jackson, who is buried in Tartaraghan Parish Churchyard.

Another John Jackson, from this area, fought with King William 111 at the Battle of the Boyne in 1690 and his sword and cutlass used in the battle have been displayed at Carrickfergus Castle in Co Antrim.

The Jacksons of Co Armagh have always been strong supporters of the Orange-Protestant cause in Ireland and today that tradition is manifested in their membership of various Orange lodges in a region, where the Orange Order was founded in 1795. These Jacksons primarily belong to the Church of Ireland (Episcopal) and, if the American link is true, it would have meant that the emigrant John Jackson and his family almost certainly converted to Presbyterianism when they reached America.

John Jackson had a brief sojourn in London before he reached Maryland in 1748. It was there that he met the wife he was to marry in America, Elizabeth Cummins, the daughter of a London hotelier, who, when her father died and her mother remarried, decided to emigrate.

Elizabeth was a highly educated woman, of a large stature and it was said she was "as remarkable for her strength of intellect as for beauty and physical vigour". Jackson was a "a spare diminutive man, of quiet, but determined character, sound judgment and excellent morals".

The pair married in 1755 and within two years they headed to the Shenandoah Valley with the great flow of Scots-Irish families who had moved from Ulster. They settled at Moorefield in Hardy County, West Virginia, but after the French-Indian War of the 1754-63 they moved 150 miles westwards to find a home at Buckhannon in Randolph county, Virginia.

In his exploits as an Indian fighter and scout, John Jackson amassed sizeable land holdings in the Shenandoah Valley and these he distributed to his eight children. The Jacksons in time became one of the leading families in the Valley, in terms of wealth and influence. Jackson was a Randolph county justice and in 1789, at the age of 74, he served as captain of a frontier militia company.

Elizabeth Jackson, who had possession of 3,000 acres of land in her own right at Buckhannon, survived her husband and lived until she was 105. She also showed tenacity and courage in fending off Indian attacks on their home and family records record that even in the most dangerous situations, she never wilted.

Two sons rose to high office. Edward (1759-1828), grandfather of "Stonewall", was Randolph county surveyor, militia colonel, commissioner of revenue and high sheriff. He represented Lewis county in the Virginia assembly and was "a citizen who acquired some knowledge of medicine, was an expert millwright and a farmer of more than usual ability".

George, his older brother, after service as a colonel in the Revolutionary War, completed three terms in the American Congress and was a close associate of General Andrew Jackson, later to become President. George and Andrew Jackson were not related, but they frequently talked about their first generation Ulster connections who had moved to America several decades earlier. George Jackson's son, John George Jackson replaced his father in Congress and, as a lawyer, he was an articulate spokesman in Washington for the Shenandoah Valley dwellers.

Jonathan Jackson, father of "Stonewall", studied law at the Clarksburg office of his uncle and, although he married the daughter of a merchant from Parslbury, West Virginia, Julie Beeleith Neale, he was never a man of great wealth. He died when his son Thomas Jonathan was only three.

John George Jackson married Mary Payne, of Philadelphia, a sister of Dolly Madison, wife of James Madison, the fourth President of the United States. This increased the influence of the Jackson clan to the highest level and John George was appointed by Madison's successor in the White House, James Monroe, as the first federal judge for the western part of Virginia. A brother, Edward Brake Jackson, was an army surgeon during the Creek Indian War of 1812, a Clarksburg doctor and a member of the American Congress for four years.

It was from a noble family tradition of soldiering and public service that Thomas Jonathan "Stonewall" Jackson emerged and in 1842, at the age of 18, he was given a Congressional appointment to the top American military academy at West Point.

With his father leaving little property on his death and his mother forced to seek the help of her relatives and the Free Masons to rear the family before she died four years later, it was a tough upbringing for Thomas Jonathan and his brother Warren and sister Laura. When orphaned, they went to live with their father's half-brother on a western Virginia farm.

"Stonewall" was a youth of "exemplary habits, of indomitable will and undoubted courage", and, in the rough and tumble of frontier society, he demonstrated an integrity and a determination to succeed in life.

Before he enrolled at West Point, "Stonewall" was a constable in his Virginia county executing court decrees, serving warrants, summoning witnesses and collecting debts. The West Point training was far removed from the law-enforcement duties of his frontier homeland, but "Stonewall" adapted well and in 1746 he graduated, 17th in a class of 70 which contained men who were to serve as the leading generals in the Civil War, in both the Union and Confederate armies.

"Stonewall" was first assigned as a lieutenant in the Mexican War, under General Zachary Taylor, a fellow Virginian who became American President in 1849. He also fought in the Seminole Indian War in Florida and was elevated to major. However, Jackson moved away from the front line of battle in 1851 when he accepted a teaching position at the Virginia Military Institute in Lexington and, although still technically in soldiering, this brought him back into civilian life. The 10 years in Lexington was perhaps the most crucial period of his life and there he was to build a solid base for his later affray at the head of the Virginia Confederate troops in the Civil War.

Jackson, although born into a Presbyterian family, had very little religious grounding as a youth and during his early military career. This changed when he met Colonel Francis Taylor, commandant of his regiment in Mexico and a committed Christian. "Stonewall" studied the Bible for himself and curiosity about various religions even led him to the Roman Catholic archbishop of Mexico for advice. But he was not convinced by the validity of Roman Catholic doctrine and in 1849 he was baptised at the age of 25 into the Episcopal Church, the American branch of Anglicanism.

In Lexington, however, it was the Presbyterian Church - the creed of the pioneering Ulster settlers, which provided him with spiritual satisfaction and he made his profession of faith as a dissenting Calvinist in November, 1851. Soon after he became a Presbyterian elder, and a lay preacher with intent to win souls for Christ.

"Stonewall" married Eleanor Junkin, daughter of the Rev George Junkin, president of Washington College in Virginia in 1854, but she died 14 months into the marriage. His second marriage in 1857, was to Mary Anna Morrison, daughter of the Rev Dr R. H. Morrison, President of Davidson College in North Carolina. They had one daughter.

Religion was the main pre-occupation for Stonewall in those Lexington years, and he daily took the Bible as his guide, literally interpreting every word on its pages. He was a strict Sabbatarian - never reading a letter on that day, nor posting one; he believed that the federal government in carrying the mail on Sundays was violating a divine law.

To the church, Jackson gave one-tenth of his income, established a Sunday school from his own means and was particularly compassionate about the plight of the black slave children in the area. Jackson's faith transcended every action of his life. He started the day with a blessing and always ended it with thanks to God. His watchword was:

"I have long cultivated the most trivial and customary acts of life with a silent prayer".

His two wives, during their marriages, were of similar fundamentalist Christian outlook, both daughters of the Presbyterian manse. Eleanor Junkin' father was of Scottish Covenanting stock, who had come from Ulster in the late 18th century. The Morrisons were also of Scots-Irish extraction.

Jackson was not a wealthy man, notwithstanding his senior position at Lexington Military College. He depended solely on his salary and both his wives were also of limited means. But he still managed to extend traditional Virginian hospitality to all who came in contact with him.

When the Civil War broke out in April, 1861 and Virginia was seceded from the Union, "Stonewall" answered the Confederate call to action and was commissioned a colonel. He led a detachment of Virginia Military Institute cadets from Lexington to Richmond to defend the Confederate flank there. This led to the command of the Virginian forces at Harper's Ferry, a posting that placed him in the front line.

Jackson distinguished himself at the Battle of Bull Run at Manassas in July, 1861, when he inflicted a crushing defeat on the Union Army. The bravery was such that General Bernard E. Bee, commander of the South Carolina Confederacy, cried out to his men to look to Jackson, stating: "There he stands like a stone wall. Rally behind the Virginians". Bee, Jackson's classmate from West Point, died in the battle, but the "Stonewall" tribute became a legend.

At the second Battle of Bull Run in August, 1862, "Stonewall" furthered distinguished himself by his valour. After marching 51 miles in two days, his "foot cavalry" smashed the Union depot at Manassas, went underground for another two days, and then held off superior forces until Confederate reinforcements could be called. He also had notable battle success at Harper's Valley, Antietam-Sharpsbury and Fredericksburg.

"Stonewall" Jackson sadly had his last stand at the Battle of Chancellorsville on May 2, 1863 and the outstanding contribution he and his men made there ensured victory for General Robert E. Lee. However, the advantage from the victory was not to last as the tide gradually turned against the Confederates, due to lack of money and resources.

After his heroics at Bull Run, Jackson was upgraded to Major-General and placed in charge of the Confederate Army in the lower Shenandoah Valley. His soldiers referred to him as "Old Jack" and his tall, thin, frame and long beard belied his barely 40 years. He remained a main of puritan tastes, a non-smoker,   non-drinker and non-gambler and he ate sparingly. His commitment to the Confederacy was total and in uniform was a stern disciplinarian, but he looked on war as "the sum of all evil".

Jackson moved to attack the Union forces in the Valley and, while they had reversals, they managed to hold the line and send the enemy retreating back to Washington. It was at Chancellorsville that Jackson was the victim of mistaken fire by one of his own men. He lost an arm after being struck three times and was forced to retire from the battle-field. Death followed quickly when he contacted pneumonia, but in a final order "Stonewall" called out: "Pass the infantry to the front".

His last words underlined his abiding Christian faith: "Let us cross over the river and rest under the shade of the trees".

Thomas Jonathan "Stonewall" Jackson was only 39 when he died on May 10, 1863. General Robert E. Lee, who had lost his finest soldier, said: "I know not how to replace him". Jackson was much respected even by enemy officers on the Union side for his heroism, bravery, devotion to duty and purity of character. He was the true Christian patriot and President Abraham Lincoln, who died within two years, described him as a "a very brave soldier".

Jackson's death two years into the Civil War has fuelled debate as to what might have happened if he had lived. Serious reversals in the Shenandoah Valley and at Gettysburg sealed the fate of the Confederacy for without the sterling leadership qualities of the redoubtable "Stonewall", the Johnny Rebs were never the same potent force again. Economic factors also seriously negated their war effort.

The heroics in battle of the gallant "Stonewall" Jackson were in the best Scots-Irish tradition - he was a soldier of very special quality.

*Thomas Jonathan "Stonewall" Jackson at the Battle of Bull
Run. It was here he acquired his famous nickname
"Stonewall".*

20

JEB Stuart - *Confederate hero in the Shenandoah Valley*

James Ewell Brown ("JEB") Stuart was another distinguished Confederate general in the American Civil War whose 18th century family descendants were Ulster Presbyterians. The gallant Stuart was the great, great, grandson of Archibald Stuart, who emigrated from Londonderry to Pennsylvania in 1726 and was one of the earliest settlers in the Shenandoah Valley of Virginia.

JEB Stuart was described by General Robert E. Lee as "the eyes of the Confederacy" and in the Virginia campaign he became a real thorn in the flesh for the Union command, leading raid after raid on their posts and taking hundreds of prisoners back to the South.

When "Stonewall" Jackson was killed at Chancellorsville in May, 1863, the imposing Stuart took over temporary command, but General Lee maintained he was irreplaceable as the Confederates' chief of calvary and he kept him in that position.

Stuart, a graduate of West Point military college and a soldier who served with the US cavalry in Texas and Kansas, resigned his commission to join the Confederate army at the start of the Civil War and he rose from second lieutenant to major general. He was a strongly religious man in the Calvinist tradition and a strong advocate of temperance, but he was of a fiery disposition which brought him into occasional conflict with his peers at West Point and which he harnessed to good effect in the various Civil War battles.

Stuart inherited his undoubted fighting qualities from stout Presbyterian kinsfolk who fought at the Siege of Londonderry in

1688-89 after they had settled arrived from lowland Scotland during the 17th century Scottish plantation of Ulster. Archibald Stuart was followed to America by his wife Janet Brown and two young children Thomas and Eleanor. Two other children Alexander and Benjamin were born in Pennsylvania and in 1737 the family set up home in Augusta county in the Shenandoah Valley.

Janet Brown's brother was the Rev John Brown, minister of Providence Presbyterian Church in Rockbridge county, Virginia for 44 years and the second rector of Liberty Hall Academy, now Washington and Lee University in Lexington.

Alexander Stuart was a major in the Virginia militia during the Revolutionary War and he later acquired extensive properties throughout the Shenandoah Valley. This land was distributed among the 11 children of his three marriages when he died in 1824, aged 90.

Thomas Stuart inherited his father's main estate in Rockbridge country and with it, the large family Bible, which had been taken from Londonderry in 1726. Eleanor, Archibald's only daughter, married Edward Hall, who was also born in Ulster and had moved to the Shenandoah Valley with his family. She and her brother Benjamin were also given farms from the prosperous estate of their father.

Judge Alexander Stuart, a son of Major Alexander Stuart and Mary Moore Paxton (Stuart's second marriage) was a lawyer, a member of the executive council of Virginia and a United States judge in Illinois and Missouri. He is buried beside his half-brother Judge Archibald Stuart, from the marriage of Major Stuart and Mary Patterson, Judge Alexander Stuart married Anne Dabney, from a family of French immigrants, and they had a son Archibald and daughter Anne.

This Archibald Stuart was the father of James Ewell Brown Stuart and his other six sons and four daughters were prominent in business, church, civic and political life in Virginia and surrounding states.

JEB Stuart as a colonel of the First Virginia Cavalry, fought at Fort Manassas-Bull Run, leading his troops in the charge which secured a significant Confederate victory. He set out detailed plans for the Virginia campaign and got behind enemy lines for an assessment of Union army strengths. This took him to the Potomac region and he returned to the Shenandoah Valley base with 165 prisoners and 260 captured horses.

His promotion to major general placed Stuart in charge of all the cavalry in Northern Virginia and, in another ambitious foray into Union territory with 1,800 troopers, he returned with 500 captured horses. JEB's daring exploits became the talk of the South and his men took inspiration from his fearlessness and willingness to take on any assignment for the Confederate cause.

This huge frame of a man with a flowing beard, invariably led from the front, nearly always astride a magnificent charger. His dashing demeanour manifested itself in his long grey Confederate coat, trimmed in red and a cavalier's cocked hat with a gilt star and a long peacock's plume. JEB enjoyed music and dancing, and, socially, he was the life and soul of the party. But he had a strong aversion to alcohol and discouraged his men against its consumption.

Stuart and his Virginia cavalry continued to act as a buffer and intelligence unit for Lee's main army, but they had their set-backs, particularly at the Battle of Gettysburg, the real turning point in the Civil War.

Stuart's cavalry covered Lee's movements during the Wilderness campaign of May, 1864 and he led 4,500 troopers in pursuit of the 12,000 Federal Cavalry Corps, commanded by Co Cavan (Ireland)-born general Philip Henry Sheridan. The Confederate cavalry reached Yellow Station on the Richmond Road and, while they succeeded in moving the Union troops off the main route to Washington, Stuart was a casualty. He was shot in the abdomen and died from his injuries in Richmond the following day, aged only 31.

General Robert E. Lee, in a tribute, said: "JEB Stuart never brought me a false piece of information. He was a gallant soldier and a fine Southerner."

JEB Stuart was married to Flora Cooke, daughter of Philip George Cooke, a general in the United States army, but a native of Virginia and a Confederate sympathiser. They had two children JEB (James Elwell Brown) and Virginia Pelham.

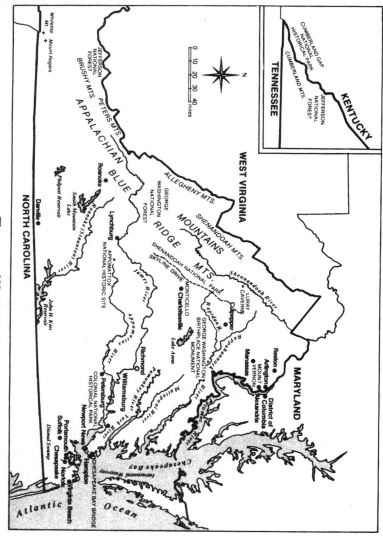

The state of Virginia.

21

Woodrow Wilson - *far-seeing American President who staked a lot for world peace*

Thomas Woodrow Wilson was not a soldier whose heroics could be assessed on the battle field, but as the American President during the First World War he was called upon to display a certain type of courage in the face of German aggression, and for his stand in pursuit of world peace he was awarded the Nobel Peace prize.

Under Woodrow Wilson's leadership during two Presidential terms from 1913 to 1921, America became a world super power and right across the states industry and commerce flourished. American historians have generally ranked Democrat Woodrow Wilson one of their great Presidents, behind Abraham Lincoln and Thomas Jefferson, but alongside Andrew Jackson, Theodore Roosevelt and Franklin D. Roosevelt. In an address to Congress in 1917, Wilson said: "There must be, not a balance of power, but a community of power, not organised rivalries, but an organised common peace."

Herbert Hoover, a Republican successor in the White House, said: "Three qualities of greatness stood out in Woodrow Wilson. He was a man of staunch morals. He was more than just an idealist; he was the personification of the idealism of the American people. He brought spiritual concepts to the peace table. He was a born crusader".

Wilson, of course, was a third generation Scots-Irishman, whose grandfather James Wilson emigrated from Strabane in Co Tyrone in 1807 after having worked at the Gray's Shop printing house where John Dunlap, who printed the Declaration of Independence in 1776, was an employee. Woodrow Wilson's other grandfather the Rev

Thomas Woodrow was a Scottish Presbyterian minister and his own father Joseph Ruggles Wilson was a minister of the Church in Staunton, Virginia.

Woodrow Wilson spoke often about his Scots-Irish family roots, and remarked that he had inherited the stern, strongly independent characteristics of the Scottish Covenanters. As the President of Princeton University in 1909, he told a St Patrick's Day rally in New York: "I myself am happy that there runs in my veins a very considerable strain of Irish blood, and a Scottish conscience."

In 1913, the year after he was elected to a first term as a Democratic President, Wilson said: "My father's father was born in the north of Ireland, he had no brothers on this side of the water. The family came from the neighbourhood, I have understood as Londonderry."

Wilson, who was Governor of New Jersey for two years before he became President, once described his nature as a struggle between his Irish blood - "quick, generous, impulsive, anxious always to help and to sympathise with those in distress" and his Scottish blood - "canny, tenacious, and perhaps a little exclusive".

When the First World War began in 1914, Woodrow Wilson advised that the United States should remain strictly neutral, but public opinion in the States gradually changed, shaped by natural affiliations to the former European homelands, and as a result of German hostility, including the sinking in 1915 of the British liner Lusitania off the southern coast of Ireland, which claimed 1,200 lives, 120 of them American passengers.

It was not until April, 1917 that America became officially engaged in the War and it was the intervention on the side of Britain and the Allies spelled defeat for the Germans. However, American short war involvement came at a heavy price with 300,000 US soldiers casualties.

In 1914, Wilson formulated the famous "Fourteen Points" which he felt would make the world "safe for democracy" and he led the American delegation at the Paris Peace Convention of 1919, and he played a leading role in compiling the Treaty of Versailles, which placed total blame on the Germans for the War. The League of Nations was formed as a result of the talks, but Wilson was prevented from having this ratified in the American Senate because it lacked a clause to guarantee US supremacy on war votes.

President Wilson's Presidential terms coincided with the years of the bitter political struggle in Ireland, but despite intense pressure on him from Irish American elements within the Democratic Party to intevene on behalf of the Irish nationalist cause he wisely decided not to get involved. He saw the Irish question purely as an internal British matter and did not perceive the dispute and unrest in Ireland as comparable to the plight of the various nationalities in Europe as a result of the fall-out from the First World War.

Wilson ignored a letter from Irish nationalist leaders in Dublin in 1918 calling on the United States to back moves for the disengagement of British interests in Ireland. The nationalist letter was countered by a communique from Ulster Unionist leaders in the north of Ireland, including Sir Edward Carson, but the President decided that American involvement was inappropriate.

Woodrow Wilson visited Ireland in August, 1899 during his period as a professor of jurisprudence and political economy at Princeton University. He is understood to have made it to Belfast, but the only evidence of his trip is contained in a letter located amongst his personal papers. This was written on August 20 from the White Horse Inn at Drogheda in Co Louth, about 25 miles south of the present Irish border.

He wrote home: "Crowds both on board the boat from England and in Dublin for the Dublin Horse Show have decided me to make my journey northward at once and by rail, asking chance acquaintances on the boat where I should go to; and therefore I am in Drogheda. I don't clearly know yet exactly where Drogheda is. I have not been to find a map to look it up yet. I only know that it is north of Dublin. But it's not on me to repine just now. This the last letter before I come myself. I sail Saturday".

Woodrow Wilson, at the time, would have been largely unknown in Ireland, north or south, and it is thought unlikely he would have travelled from Dublin or Belfast to North Tyrone to trace his family roots.

Religion played a big part in Woodrow Wilson's life; he often proclaimed that his faith was pure and simple. "Never for a moment have I had one doubt about my religious beliefs," he asserted. A strong Calvinist, Wilson read his Bible daily, said grace before meals and prayed on his knees each morning and evening. He believed in providence and predestination and that God had foreordained him as President. He worshipped at Central Presbyterian Church in Washington.

Wilson, who died in 1924 aged 67, was married twice. His first wife was Ellen Louise Axson, from Savannah, Georgia and, when she died 29 years into the marriage, he wed widower Edith Bolling Galt, who survived him by 37 years.

Woodrow Wilson, in one of his final speeches, said: "Sometimes, people call me an idealist. Well that is the way I know I am an American. America, my fellow citizens, I do not say in disparagement of any other great people, but America is the only idealistic nation in the world". Patriotic words from a President so proud of his heritage!

The Scots-Irish from Ulster became pioneers and frontiersmen of early America, clearing the forests to make their farms and living in log cabins such as the one depicted above.

22

"Big Foot" Wallace - *Texas Ranger and mail carrier on the Tex/Mex border*

William Alexander Anderson Wallace, known as 'Big Foot', was a Shenandoah Valley-born Texas Ranger, hunter and adventurer, who fought with distinction against the Mexicans and Indians in the San Antonio area during the conflict of the 1840s.

'Big Foot' was the great grandson of Ulster Presbyterian couple Peter and Elizabeth Wallace and his memory is perpetuated on a bronze statue in the centre of Lexington, Virginia.

The statue bears the inscription: "Big Foot Wallace 1817-99. William Alexander Wallace was born one mile south of this corner marker in a brick house still standing, which was near the dwelling of his grandfather Samuel Wallace, where the first Rockbridge Court was held in 1778. At the age of 23, he went to Texas in 1837 to avenge the death of his brother, who were massacred by the Mexicans at Goliad". A cousin also died at Goliad.

"Wallace served his adopted state as an Indian fighter, Ranger, Civil War soldier and post carrier, enduring great hardship and ordeals recorded in history. His remains are interred in San Antonio and the state of Texas has signally honoured his memory. Wallace motto - Sperandum. Erected by his Virginia and Texas admirers. 1935."

'Big Foot' was a trouble shooter, operating from a San Antonio base. He would gather up small parties of men to cover a radius of 40 miles from San Antonio wherever hostile Indians were reported and his function was to meet danger head on. He had many violent run-ins with the Indian tribes and fought the Mexicans at the battle of Meir.

More than 600 Mexicans were killed at Meir, but with rations running out the Texans surrendered and Santa Anna ordered every man to be shot. His governor Francisco Mexia, however, disobeyed and ordered every tenth man to be shot. A jar was filled with white beans and seventeen black beans.

The seventeen prisoners who drew a black bean were executed on March 25, 1843 and while many of the remaining prisoners died in captivity, "Bigfoot" Wallace was one of the few to escape and he lived to fight in the Mexican-American War and later joined the Texas Rangers.

When peace was declared, Wallace, also known as "Cap", acted as a guard or escort to the postal stage line carrying the mail between San Antonio and along the Rio Grande through old Fort Franklin, now El Paso city, and Albuquerque, New Mexico. The guards of the stage rode on horseback alongside the stage through dangerous territory inhabited by Indians and Mexican bandits.

Wallace's great grandmother Elizabeth Woods Wallace emigrated from the north of Ireland with her six children, five sons and one daughter, and four brothers and their families, after her husband Peter died in 1724. They settled at Lancaster county, Pennsylvania and moved to Rockbridge county in the Shenandoah Valley of Virginia in 1739.

The Wallace family spread out from Virginia to Kentucky and Indiana and relatives of "Big Foot" were David Wallace, a governor of Washington territory, and General Lew Wallace, a governor of New Mexico and a leading American author. General Wallace fought in the Civil War and he served on the court martial for Abraham Lincoln's assassin, John Wilkes Booth.

Another family of Wallaces, James and Eleanor McCullough Wallace from Co. Tyrone sailed with their nine children from Belfast to Charleston on the ship Lord Dungannon in 1768. This family eventually settled at Abbeville in the South Carolina Piedmont and James was a captain in the South Carolina militia in the Revolutionary War.

23

Mary and John Patton - *powder makers in the Revolutionary War*

Mary Patton was a heroine in the Appalachian backcountry for the part she played in the American Revolutionary War as gunpowder maker for the patriot army. Mary McKeehan was English-born of Scottish parentage and she married Ulster Presbyterian John Patton in 1772 after their families settled in eastern Pennsylvania.

The art of powder making was shown to Mary by her father David when they lived in England and the experience was passed on to husband John in his role as a militia man and general merchant in the Cumberland county region of Pennsylvania.

The Pattons had two children and, finding their region over-run by Redcoat soldiers, they sold their business and headed to the Sycamore Shoals-Elizabethton area of North Carolina which today is located in East Tennessee. There, in the company of Andrew Taylor, another Scots-Irish settler, they established a gunpowder mill.

Mary was the real expert when it came to powder making, simply using a large black kettle. She made 500 pounds of black gunpowder for use by the Overmountain Men from the Sycamore Shoals area, who took part in the Battle of Kings Mountain on October 7, 1780.

The potent mix was an essential ingredient in securing victory over the British for the Overmountain Men, who consisted mainly of Scots-Irish settler farmers from the Watauga community. The contribution of Mary Patton to the revolutionary war effort did not receive national acclaim, but in East Tennessee and North Carlina she is looked upon as a woman of great character and courage.

Mary taught other members of her family to manufacture gunpowder and the Patton mill continued in production in East Tennessee for upwards of 100 years. It was in used by the Confederates during the Civil War.

The processes in the manufacture of black gunpowder were the production of saltpeter and charcoal and in the cottage industry operation of the Patton household mill much hand labour was necessary. The powder was packed in 25, 50 and 100 pound kegs.

Three Pattons - Robert, Thomas and Matthew, all from a Scots-Irish background, are listed as having fought in the Battle of Kings Mountain.

Mary Patton Memorial.

24

Kate Barry - *steely heroine of the Cowpens*

Margaret Catherine (Kate) Barry, from Walnut Grove, Spartanburg in South Carolina, was one of the outstanding heroines of the Revolutionary War, for the key role she played in saving lives during the crucial Battle of Cowpens in January, 1781.

Kate, daughter of Co Antrim couple Charles and Mary Barry Moore who emigrated to America about 1750, was a women of steely character marrying, at 15, Captain Andrew Barry, who was also from a Scots-Irish family that had settled in the Tyger River region of South Carolina.

Andrew Barry was a captain in the South Carolina rangers during the War and he commanded companies at the battles of Fishing Creek, Musgrove's Mill (where he was wounded) and Cowpens. Kate and Andrew made their home on the Tyger River and they had 11 children, five sons and six daughters.

Kate was a volunteer scout and guide for the South Carolina Piedmont patriots, acting always in support of her husband. The scouting operations centred mainly in Spartanburg county and, being an excellent horse woman, able to ride side saddle, she was familiar with the thick wooded wilderness and Indian trails.

She frequently rode to where the patriots were camped to warn of impending danger and had an ally in a black slave Uncle Cato, who, when it was impossible for her to go on scouting expeditions, deputised. Kate and Uncle Cato would fill hollow trees with corn to provide against food shortage emergencies. Raids by the British forces sometimes left patriot families destitute and the corn caches in the trees were required to feed the people and their animals.

Kate was even engaged in rounding up militia troops when reinforcements were needed. At the Battle of Cowpens she took on the task of gathering up patriot bands and moving them to the frontline. There, her husband was holding the line with General Andrew Pickens against British troops, under the notorious Redcoat commander Banastre Tarleton, a Merseysider who was hated by the up-country Scots-Irish Carolina settlers for his butchery.

During the battle of Cowpens the women of Nazarath Presbyterian Church, 13 miles away, were assembled in a house near the church and the ever watchful Kate Barry was at the shoals on the Tyger River, waiting for reports from the battlefield. When informed of the crushing victory for the patriots she rushed to the women with the news. At Cowpens, 926 of Tarleton's troops were killed, captured or wounded and many armaments were taken. On the American side, 132 were killed and 60 wounded.

When the British, under "Bloody Bill" Cunningham made their infamous raid into the area, Kate heard them from across the river near her father's house at Walnut Grove. She tied her two-year-old Catherine (Little Katie) to the bed post for safety, rode to her husband's company for help, thereby forcing the British to retreat.

Once, when the Redcoats came to Kate's house demanding to know of the whereabouts of Andrew Barry's company, she refused to inform, and was tied up and struck three times with a leash. This attack angered the men of her husband's company, for it was said any one of them would have given his own life to save hers.

In another incident, with the British in hot pursuit, Kate swam her horse across the Pacolet River near Hurricane Shoals. Miraculously, the water rose to a high level just as Kate and the horse reached dry ground on the other side, thus preventing the British from capturing her and the important news that she carried.

Andrew Barry died in 1811 and Kate outlived him by 13 years. She died aged 71 and was buried in the Moore family cemetery at Walnut Grove. The heroic deeds of Kate Barry have been part of South Carolina folklore for more than 200 years and today her memory is revered by the people of the Spartanburg and Greenville area.

Kate's nephew, Senator William Taylor Barry, was President Andrew Jackson's Postmaster General in the White House, after soldiering with Jackson in the War of 1812-13. He was also US minister to Spain.

Another relative, Colonel Thomas John Moore, a grandson of Charles and Mary Moore, served in the South Carolina House of Representatives and Senate. He was a Confederate Army officer in the Civil War, serving with the 18th South Carolina Volunteers in the Carolinas and Virginia. He was imprisoned by Union forces after capture in 1865 and held until the War ended. After a pardon issued by President Andrew Johnson, Thomas Moore was appointed colonel in the 36th regiment of the South Carolina state militia.

The Craig connection with the Moores of Walnut Grove dates back to James Craig, who was born at Templepatrick, Co. Antrim in 1754 and arrived at Charleston in 1773 on board the ship Britannia. In 1777 James married Jinny Bell, born at Ahoghill, Co. Antrim in 1785. Their son Arthur Rosborough Craig married Henrietta Sue Moore, great-granddaughter of Charles and Mary Moore.

Walnut Grove, Spartanburg.

Settlement and migration of the Scots-Irish in North America.

25

Settlements in Ulster: *The Scottish Presbyterians and the French Huguenots*

THE SCOTTISH PRESBYTERIANS

Lowland Scottish Presbyterians first arrived in the north of Ireland in 1605, courtesy of Sir Arthur Chichester, the Deputy Lieutenant of Ireland, and the movement continued throughout the 17th century in what was known as the Scottish Plantation. The Church of Scotland was established in 1590 as a Presbyterian Calvinist church

The Episcopacy (or Anglican creed) was officially rejected by churchmen and the general population in Scotland in 1638, after decisions of the National Covenant, and the Glasgow Assembly, which deposed the bishops and firmly established Presbyterianism as the main denomination in the country.

When the first Presbyterian ministers came to Ireland they were kindly received by the then Church of Ireland archbishop James Ussher, whose tolerance was evidenced in the Irish Articles of Religion which showed a leaning towards Presbyterianism.

In Co Down the Scottish planter families, most prominent among them the Hamiltons and the Montgomerys, encouraged Church of Scotland ministers to settle and this led to their appointment in the incumbencies of Church of Ireland parishes. Robert Blair, who was formerly Regent of Glasgow University, became rector of Bangor; James Hamilton, a nephew of Lord Clandeboye, was appointed rector of Ballywalter; and Josias Walsh, a nephew of John Knox, was made rector of Templepatrick.

These men were scholars and from a noble background and the Church of Ireland bishops accepted them as being important in raising the religious and moral standards in the country. Other Scottish clerics who came to Ulster in the early 17th century were of more lowly backgrounds, very firm in their Calvinist faith and they set about forming congregations in various parts of the Province.

A significant chapter in the growth of Presbyterianism in Ulster came with the arrival of a 10,000-strong Scottish army under the command of General Robert Munro to put down a native Irish rebellion. The army brought along its Presbyterian chaplains and in each of the four regiments there was a Kirk Session. On June 10, 1642 the four sessions met at Carrickfergus to constitute the first presbytery in Ireland and the Scottish influence on Irish Presbyterianism had begun.

From this moment the Presbyterian Church in Ireland took on the shape and form that it has now, with its ministers, elders, congregations and ecclesiastical courts working in the most democratic system. Today, Presbyterianism is the largest Protestant denomination in Northern Ireland with up to half a million adherents, but its strength would certainly have doubled had several hundred thousand Presbyterians not emigrated to America during the 18th century.

THE FRENCH HUGUENOTS

The Huguenots originate from a group of Calvinist Protestants who were persecuted in France during the 16th and 17th centuries and fled from the strictures of the Roman Catholic Church, which was so dominant in French life at the time.

Many Huguenots went to Holland, Switzerland, Germany and Denmark, with about 40,000 coming to Britain (10,000 of them opting to live in Ireland!). An act in the British parliament allowed the Huguenots to become naturalised citizens and freemen of towns and guilds and a Huguenot colony of linen workers was set up in Dublin and another of wool workers at Clonmel in Co Tipperary.

A sizeable Huguenot community settled in the Lagan Valley around Lisburn in Co Antrim and there they set up the linen industry and played a major role in the civic, business and agricultural life of the region. Belfast was also a town where the Huguenots had influence during the 18th century   .

Two Huguenot congregations existed in Dublin and, after the victory of King William 111 at the Battle of the Boyne in 1690, they were accorded a degree of religious toleration that was greater than that of Presbyterian dissenters and Roman Catholics.

The best-known Huguenot was the Duke of Schomberg, the second in command of William 111, who was killed in action at the Battle of the Boyne. Other Huguenots of distinction were James Gandon, architect of the Custom House and the Four Courts in Dublin, and Richard Cassels, the architect of Leinster House, the Retounda Hospital and Trinity College in Dublin.

The leading private bank, La Toche, was started by a Huguenot who had a poplin factory before coming to Ireland with King William and soldiering at the Boyne. His grandson was the first governor of the Bank of Ireland when it was founded in 1783.

Many Huguenots, who fought in the Williamite Wars in Ireland, settled in Belfast, assimilating either into the Church of Ireland or the Presbyterian Church. In later years, the General Assembly of the Presbyterian Church in Ireland when paying tribute to the worth of the Huguenots expressed regret that coming from the Reformed Church in France so many had joined the Church of Ireland (Episcopal) rather than the Presbyterian Church.

A number of Huguenot families joined the Ulster Presbyterians in the emigration to America in the 18th century, while others had travelled direct to the colonies after being ejected from France in the late 17th century. They settled mainly in Pennsylvania, New York, Virginia and South Carolina.

There they became heavily involved in business life and in the organisation of the Reformed and Presbyterian churches. New York and Charleston were American cities that built up strong Huguenot influences.

The American frontiersman (painting by David Wright, Nashville).

26

Important correspondence: *Andrew Jackson's poignant letter written on a tragic day and David Crockett's last letter home*

Andrew Jackson wrote a letter from his Hermitage, Nashville home to his doctor at Tallahassee in Florida, General Richard Keith Call, on the serious condition of his wife Rachel. Poignantly, the letter was written on Sunday December 22, 1828, just hours before Rachel died and the contents indicate the real extent and life-threatening nature of her illness.

"Mrs J. was a few days past, suddenly and violently attacked, with pains in her left shoulder, and breast and such was the contraction of the breast, that suffocation was apprehended before the necessary aid could be afforded. Doctor Hogg has relieved her and, although worse today than yesterday, I trust in a kind providence, that he will restore her to her usual health in due time to set out for Washington, so that I may reach there by the middle of February.

"We have been waiting to hear from you, in hopes you may reach us before we set out, which will be between the 10th and 15th of January - should the Ohio keep open we will go by water to Wheeling or Pittsburgh. Mrs J. situation will make this route necessary, as I am fearful that her strength would not be able to undergo the journey overland, and I cannot leave her, believing that as I do that my separating from her would destroy her, and the persecution she has suffered has endeared her more if possible than ever to me.

"The little junto of calumniators here have found their level, the verdict which has been pronounced against them by the people, has taught them that truth is mighty and will prevail, and calumniators will meet the just abhorrence of a virtuous people. I need not assure of the pleasure it will afford me and Mrs J. to meet you at the city, should you not arrive at The Hermitage before we set out. Mrs J., who is confined to her bed, unites with me in a tender of our kindest salutations and good wishes to you, Mrs Call and the sweet little ones. Believe me your friend.

Andrew Jackson."

The letter was received Dr Call in Florida on December 27.

* Rachel Jackson never made it to the White House in Washington to attend the inauguration of her husband Andrew for his first term as President. She died from her illness on December 22, 1828, after suffering the personal anguish of direct attacks on her character during the Presidential campaign because a previous marriage to Lewis Robards, of Kentucky, had not been officially annulled when she married Jackson.

DAVY CROCKETT'S LAST LETTER HOME

Seven weeks before Davy Crockett's death at The Alamo he wrote his last letter. The letter, written from Nacogdoches, Texas on January 15, 1836, was to his daughter Margaret (Polly) and her husband Wiley Flowers: "My dear son and daughter, I am now blessed with excellent health and am in high spirits. I have got through safe and have been received by everybody with the ceremony of friendship. I am hailed with a hearty welcome to this country. A dinner and party of ladys have honored me with an invitation.

"The cannon was fired here on my arrival and I must say as to what I have seen of Texas it is the garden spot of the world, the best land and the best prospects for good health I ever saw and I do believe it is a fortune to any man to come here. There is a world of country to settle, the richest country in the world. Good land, plenty of timber and the best springs and good mill streams, good range of clear water . . . game aplenty.

"I have taken the oath of government and have enrolled my name as volunteer for six months and will set out for the Rio Grande in a few days with the volunteers. I am rejoiced at my fate. I had rather be in my present situation than to be elected to a seat in Congress for life.

I am in hopes of making a fortune yet for myself and family. I hope you will all do the best you can and I will do the same. Do not be uneasy about me. I am among friends,

Your affectionate father. Farewell David Crockett!"

SCOTS-IRISH PRESIDENTS

Thirteen of the 41 Presidents of the United States have direct family links to the north of Ireland and the Scots-Irish immigrants who moved to America in the 18th century and early 19th century. Three of these Presidents also served as Vice-Presidents, with a fourth, John C. Calhoun, occupying the No. 2 position in the White House for two terms.

PRESIDENTS OF THE UNITED STATES

- ★ **Andrew Jackson (1829-37).** Democrat. Co. Antrim stock.
- ★ **James Knox Polk (1845-49).** Democrat. Co. Londonderry/ Co. Donegal stock.
- ★ **James Buchanan (1857-61).** Democrat. Co. Donegal stock.
- ★ **Andrew Johnson (1865-69).** Democrat. Co. Antrim stock.
- ★ **Ulysses Simpson Grant (1869-77).** Republican. Co. Tyrone stock.
- ★ **Chester Alan Arthur(1881-85).** Republican. Co. Antrim stock.
- ★ **Grover Cleveland (1885-89 and 1893-97).** Democrat. Co. Antrim stock.
- ★ **Benjamin Harrison (1889-93).** Republican. Co. Antrim stock.
- ★ **William McKinley (1897-1901).** Republican. Co. Antrim stock.
- ★ **Woodrow Wilson (1913-21).** Democrat. Co. Tyrone stock.
- ★ **Richard Millhouse Nixon (1969-74).** Republican. Co. Antrim stock.
- ★ **James Earl Carter (1976-81).** Democrat. Co. Antrim stock.

★ **William Jefferson Clinton (1993-2000).** Democrat. Co. Fermanagh stock.

Six of these Presidents were Presbyterians (Jackson, Polk, Buchanan, Cleveland, Harrison and Wilson), three were Methodists (Johnson, Grant and McKinley), with two Baptists (Carter and Clinton), one Episcopalian (Arthur) and one Quaker (Nixon).

Three other Presidents are also claimed to have Ulster connections - Theodore Roosevelt, Harry Truman and George Bush. Roosevelt's links were to East Antrim, Truman's pioneering Missouri family are thought to have Scots-Irish connections and George Bush's ancestor William Gault was a first citizen of Tennessee, very probably of Ulster origin.

VICE-PRESIDENTS OF THE UNITED STATES

★ **John C. Calhoun (1825-32).** Democrat. Co. Donegal/ Co. Londonderry stock.
★ **Andrew Johnson (1865).** Democrat. Co. Antrim stock.
★ **Chester Alan Arthur (1881).** Republican. Co. Antrim stock.
★ **Richard Millhouse Nixon (1953-61).** Republican. Co. Antrim stock.

\# Andrew Johnson became President on the assassination of President Abraham Lincoln in 1865.
\# Chester Alan Arthur became President on the assassination of President James A. Garfield in 1881.
\# President William McKinley was assassinated in 1901.

27

Generals Burnside and McClennan
of the Union Army

A mbrose Everett Burnside, the highly colourful Union general in the American Civil War and United States Senator, was of Co Antrim Presbyterian stock who had moved from Argyllshire in Scotland to Ulster during the 17th century Plantation years.

The Burnsides lived at Macfin-Seacon near Ballymoney in the Route area of North Antrim with tenant farmer James Burnside being the earliest traceable member of the clan in the region. James had four sons Samuel, Thomas, David, James and a daughter Elizabeth, with Thomas emigrating to America in 1718 with a group of Presbyterians from the Bann Valley, a 25-square mile area that covered Ballymoney, Coleraine, Macosquin, Aghadowey and Ballyrashane.

The Bann Valley Presbyterians settled in the Londonderry township of New Hampshire and Thomas Burnside Jun. (1735-1798) married Susan MacGregor, the grand-daughter of the Rev John MacGregor, the Presbyterian minister who had led the group from Ulster. David, a brother of Thomas, was drowned in the Delaware River in 1761.

The Burnsides, described as honest, independent folk, were eventually located in the Laurens area of South Carolina with other Scots-Irish immigrants and at the commencement of the Revolutionary War a Robert Burnside, believed to be Ambrose Everett's grandfather, publicly declared for the Crown.

When Robert died just after the War, son James and his wife and children moved to Jamaica to avoid the persecution that was then rampant for supporters of the loyalist cause. A few years later when the political animosities subsided they returned to continue a pioneering life in the Carolina Piedmont.

James Burnside died in 1798, leaving seven sons and two daughters, and his widow, the daughter of a Tory colonel, sought to improve the family's situation by moving to the new Indiana territory.

Other members of the family moved to Illinois and Wisconsin but Edghill, Ambrose Everett's father, made his stake in the Indiana town of Liberty with wife Pamelia Brown, daughter of another Scots-Irish settler.

There, the family (the couple had nine children!) lived in modest circumstances and Ambrose Everett, the fourth child born in 1824, was because of lack of money unable to go to college after graduation from the local seminary in Laurens.

Ambrose Everett Burnside worked as a tailor's apprentice and, largely through his father's political influence as an Indiana senator, he obtained an appointment to West Point military academy. He graduated in 1847, 18th in a class of 38 cadets, most of whom were to become leading players on the Civil War stage within a decade and a half, including a close friend George Brinton McClellan, who was also from a Scots-Irish family.

Burnside saw action on the frontier against Indian aggression, serving in the garrison of Fort Adams in Rhode Island, but in 1853 he resigned his commission to open a factory for the production of a breechloading carbine rifle he had invented. This venture only lasted a few years and he took up a post as treasurer of the Illinois Central Railroad.

When the war commenced Burnside organised the first Rhode Island regiment and he commanded a brigade at the first Battle of Bull Run in July, 1861.

Burnside, six feet tall and whose flamboyant whiskers gave the word "sideburns" to the language, was an amiable man who encompassed a wide circle of friends, including President Abraham Lincoln and his high-level connections brought him rapid advancement in the Union Army.

By February, 1862, Burnside was in charge of land forces, moving first to take Roanoke Island in North Carolina, New Bern and Beaufort

Ambrose Everett Burnside

during a two-month campaign, and by September of that year he was operating alongside George Brinton McClellan in Virginia.

In November, Lincoln relieved McClellan and put Ambrose Everett Burnside in his place as commander of the Army of the Potomac. This was a posting Burnside felt he was not qualified for, and events were to prove him correct. He reluctantly agreed to take the command, but made it clear it was not a matter of congratulations.

He was in turn relieved after losing the Battle of Fredericksburg to General Robert E. Lee in December and the January aftermath "Mud March" in which Union troops became totally bogged down in rain-sodden ground.

In March, 1863, Burnside took charge of the department of the Ohio and launched offensive operations against the Confederates behind the fighting line. In May he caused controversy by arresting former Congressman Clement Vallandigham, a prominent Democratic politician, and he also suppressed the Chicago Times newspaper, actions Lincoln had to repudiate.

Burnside did attain a significant measure of success with military operations in his department. He led the army of the Ohio to Knoxville, Tennessee in September, 1863, withstood a siege there and, after repulsing a general assault, saw the Confederates retreat from the region early in December.

In the spring of 1864, Burnside was back in Virginia as a corps commander under Generals Ulysses S. Grant and George Gordon Meade. He led the 1X Corps in the battles of The Wilderness, Spotsylvania, Cold Harbor and Petersburg in May and June.

Ambrose Everett Burnside has been heavily criticised by historians for needlessly throwing away thousands of lives in bloody battles like Fredericksburg and Petersburg, but others claim he was often the scapegoat of his superiors and junior officers.

His courage as a soldier and integrity as a person was never in doubt. His military standing is recognised by the fact that a large portrait of Ambrose Everett Burnside hangs today in the officers' mess at West Point.

"Ambrose Everett Burnside was pre-eminently a manly man. His large, fine eyes, his winning smile and cordial manners bespoke a frank, sincere and honourable character," wrote an Union Army officer who served with him.

After the War, Burnside became a successful businessman, holding the presidency of two railroad companies and a steamship company. He spent three years as state governor of Rhode Island in 1866, 1866 and 1867 and served in the United States Senate as the Rhode Island representative from 1875 until his death in September, 1881, aged only 57.

Burnside was introduced to the Senate standing alongside President Lincoln's two Vice-Presidents Hannibal Hamlin and Andrew Johnson.

Politically, Burnside was a Democrat in his early years, but he moved to the Republican Party during the Civil War and one of his main campaigning issues was support for a bill allowing black applicants special admission privileges at West Point, which was effectively an affirmative action plan.

Unlike many Republicans of the time, Burnside resumed cordial relations with former Confederates. They were always welcome at his Washington rooms, and he did nor shirk from defending them in the Senate.

George Brinton McClellan was the son of a Philadelphia surgeon, whose Ulster-Scots forebears fought alongside George Washington in the Revolutionary War. McClellan, a West Point associate of both Thomas Jonathan "Stonewall" Jackson and Ambrose Everett Burnside, entered the Civil War as a Mexican war veteran.

Like Burnside, he worked for the railway companies in Illinois, as an engineer and administrator and when war broke out he was commissioned a major general of the Ohio Volunteers and fought the Confederate in West Virginia.

His prowess as a soldier and military organiser impressed Abraham Lincoln and he was asked to reverse the set-back suffered at the first Battle of Bull Run in 1861. He strengthened the Washington and Virginia defences, but after a sustained battle with Robert E. Lee at Richmond in May-June, 1862 he was forced to retreat.

Lincoln demoted McClellan to No 2 in favour of General John Pope, but after another defeat at the second Battle of Bull Run in August, 1862, he resumed command. The general, known to his men as "Little Mac" held the line at Antietam Creek in Maryland in November, 1862, but when he failed to stop the Confederates returning to Virginia he was again removed by Lincoln.

Ironically, General Robert E. Lee considered him the ablest Union commander he had faced, but Lincoln's view was that he always wanted more men, more equipment, more time to plan. "George McClellan is an admirable engineer, but he seems to have the special talent for the stationary engine," said the President.

George Brinton McClellan

McClellan was the Democratic candidate for the Presidency against Abraham Lincoln in 1864, but he only won majority support in three states. He served for three years in 1878-81 as governor of New Jersey.

* The Burnside family connection is still evident today in the North Antrim area, with Northern Ireland politician David Burnside being a direct descendant of General Ambrose Everett. He retains possession of the General's ceremonial sword.

The family have at various times been orthodox Presbyterians, Non-Subscribing Presbyterians and Reformed Presbyterians.

28

James Adair - *genuine friend of the Indian people*

The Scots-Irish and the native American Indian tribes were for the most part during the early pioneering years of the American frontier not friendly disposed to one another and much blood was spilled on both sides, mainly over land rights.

One Ulsterman who did cultivate peaceful co-existence with the Indian tribes was James Adair, who went further than most in the white settler community to try to understand the varying cultures and traditions of the red man.

Adair, born in 1709 in Co Antrim, carved a niche as a diplomat and peacemaker among the Indian tribes of the American south east which included the Cherokees, Siouans, Catawbas, Creeks, Shawnees, Choctaws, and Chickasaws.

His book, History of the American Indians, published in London in 1775, was regarded at the time as the most authoritative work on the native American tribes.

In the book Adair theorised that the Indians were descended from the lost tribes of Israel and his detailed observations provided valuable insights for ethnologists and students of 18th century literature.

The lost tribes theory many not have been universally shared, although some writers and commentators at the time did propound the view in books and pamphlets. One early 17th century writer Garcia claimed to have found many Hebrew features in the native American languages, declaring that the lost tribes passed Behring Strait and made their way southward on the American continent.

Adair emigrated to America in 1735 and, from his tavern at Cherokee Creek in South Carolina, he traded with the Indians and from years of close hand working managed to penetrate their society, from a position of mutual trust.

He recorded Indian manners, customs and language from a standpoint that had not been been seen before by a white man. Adair lived for seven years with the Overhill (or Western) Cherokees Indians in the Tennessee River territory and in 1744 he moved to the Mississippi to reside with the Chickasaw tribes, whose influence extended down the Savannah River into North George and South Carolina.

James Adair looked on the "Chikkasah" as cheerful and brave people. He was impressed by their independence and bravery and they reciprocated the friendship. The Chickasaws disliked the French and Adair even joined them in encounters against the Shawnee, who were then aligned with the French and came to grief during the French-Indian Wars.

Accounts of Adair describe him as a man of liberal education with a sound knowledge of the Hebrew language. His diplomacy was a strong point, but his acridity of speech, an unsmooth temper and a vain spirit brought him into conflict with his white contemporaries.

James Adair recognised in the Chickasaws "love of the land, constancy in hatred and friendship, sagacity, alertness and consummate intrepidity".

A manuscript of his book published in 1775 came to light in the South Carolina Gazette on September 7, 1769. This stated: "An account of the origin of the primitive inhabitants and a history of those numerous warlike tribes of Indians, situated to the westward of Charlestown, and subjects hitherto unattempted by any pen.

"Such an attempt has been made by Mr James Adair, a gentleman who has been conversant among the Cherokees, Chickasaws, Choctaws, etc for thirty-odd years past; and who, by the assistance of a liberal education, has written essays on their origin, language, religion, customary methods of making war and peace etc."

The report announced that Adair was planning a trip to England to publish a book. A month later, both the South Carolina Gazette and the Savannah Georgia Gazette published Adair's prospectus of the book, for sale by subscription.

Essays were published on the origin, history, language, religion, customs, civil policy, methods of declaring and carrying out war, and of making peace, military laws, agriculture, buildings, exercise, sports, marriage and funeral ceremonies, habits, diets, temper, manners etc of "the Indians tribes of the continent of North America, particularly of the several nations or tribes of the Catawbas, Cherokees, Creeks, Chickasaws, and Choctaws, inhabiting the western parts of the colonies of Virginia, North and South Carolina, Georgia and the Tennessee territory".

In Winsor's 'Narrative and Critical History of America', James Adair's book is described as a work of great value, of much importance to students of Indian customs.

Logan, in his 'History of South Carolina', said that from Adair's book the world had derived most that is known of the manners and customs of the southern Indians.

"The book's style is exceedingly figurative and characteristic and partakes much of the idiom of the Indian dialects to which the author was so accustomed," he said.

The Shoshoni Indian guide Sacajawea signals to a part of Chinook Indians, as explorers Meriwether Lewis (standing), William Clark (in cocked hat), and York look on, in a depiction of a meeting in 1805. Picture: Lewis and Clark on the Lower Columbia by Charles Russell.

29

Ulster-born *militia heroes of Cowpens*

The Battle of Cowpens on January 17, 1781 fought on the Broad River on the southern part of South Carolina followed on from the defeat of the British at Kings Mountain by the American revolutionaries. Cowpens was another set-back for the British, with 1,000 patriot troops, under General Daniel Morgan, routing the Redcoats under Colonel Banastre Tarleton.

British losses were more than 100 killed, more than 200 wounded and 600 captured. Casualties for the militia were 12 dead and 60 wounded. The defeats at Kings Mountain, and Cowpens, solidified support in the region for the American patriotic cause and forced the British into desperate counter-manoeuvers.

As at Kings Mountain, a big proportion of the militia soldiers were Scots-Irish Presbyterian settlers from the Carolina Piedmont area - some native-born Ulstermen, others of first, second and third generation from immigrants from the north of Ireland.

Known Ulster-born militiamen at Cowpens were:

- **COLONEL ELIAS ALEXANDER.** Born north of Ireland 1749. Alexander's regiment of troops was very effective before and after the invasion of British troops led by Lord Charles Cornwallis in suppressing and keeping the Tories at bay. He fought at the battles of Ramsour's Mill, Kings Mountain, Cowpens and Guilford Courthouse.

- **JAMES ALEXANDER.** Born north of Ireland 1761. Recruited in the Spartanburg (South Carolina) militia and earned a reputation as an Indian fighter and undercover scout. He was involved in battles at Hollinsworth Mills, Grindal Shoals and Ninety Six.

- **WILLIAM ARMSTRONG.** Born north of Ireland 1765. A settler of the Fairfield, South Carolina district, William became a Revolutionary War veteran while still in his teens and he saw action at Rocky Mount, Bratton's Plantation and Hanging Rock, before going on to Kings Mountain and Cowpens.

- **MOSES BEARD.** Born north of Ireland 1759. A recruit from Kershaw county, South Carolina he also fought at Rocky Mount and Hanging Rock.

- **JOHN BOYCE.** Born north of Ireland about 1740. Boyce settled at Newberry, South Carolina and he was wounded in an attempt to storm Savannah. He took part in the battles of Kings Mountain, Cowpens, Blackstock's Plantation and Eutaw Springs.

- **GERARD BRANDON.** Born Co Donegal. Brandon led a cavalry charge at Kings Mountain and fought at Cowpens. He moved to West Florida, and Mississippi, where his son G. C. was the governor.

- **JOHN BUCHANAN.** Born north of Ireland. Buchanan came to America with his brother Robert a few years before the Revolution and served as a captain in the South Carolina Regiment and was taken prisoner at the fall of Charleston. On release, he raised a militia company at Fairfield, South Carolina and was at Cowpens.

- **WILLIAM BUCHANAN.** Born north of Ireland 1762. Buchanan was brought to America when only five years and he was drafted into the militia as a sixteen-year-old while residing in Ninety Six, South Carolina. He served right through various battles in the Revolutionary War in Georgia, South Carolina and North Carolina.

- **JOHN CALDWELL.** Born near Belfast 1760. He was brought to America by his parents and, while residing at Spartanburg, South Carolina, was recruited in the militia as a substitute for his father. He first served as a scout and then as a private and was at the battle of Blackstock's Plantation, Watkin's Fort, Kings Mountain and Cowpens.

- **JAMES CARLISLE.** Born Co Monaghan, Ireland 1763. Recruited into the South Carolina militia as a 17-year-old, and, after fighting at Grindal Shoals, he served at Cowpens under General Andrew Pickens. His wife was Margaret Boles.

- **SAMUEL CLOWNEY (CLUNEY).** Born north of Ireland 1740. An express rider supplier of the militia with lead and powder during the 1780 battles, Clowney was also in the battles at Reedy River, Kings Mountain and Blackstock's Plantation.

- **JEREMIAH DIAL.** Born Ireland 1758. A settler of Newberry, South Carolina, he was in the battles of Blackstock's Plantation, Cowpens and Ninety Six. Took part in various campaigns against the Indians. His wife was Nancy Anna McDaniel.

- **COLONEL JAMES HAWTHORN.** Born Co Armagh 1750. James settled on the South Carolina frontier and along with his mother and two sisters was captured by Indians. He became a blacksmith and as a militiaman fought in various campaigns against the Indians. He rose from being a first lieutenant to captain and then colonel and trained the militia for a period. He fought in most of the battles leading up to Kings Mountain and was wounded at Cowpens. He became a very wealthy landowner, with a large farm in Kentucky. His wife was a Margaret Greene.

- **COLONEL WILLIAM HILL.** Born Belfast 1740. Hill fought at the battle of Rocky Mount, Hanging Rock (where he was wounded!), Kings Mountain and Cowpens. His wife was a Jane McCall.

- **JAMES KINCAID.** Born Belfast 1752. Kincaid emigrated to Charleston and when he joined the militia when he moved up into the South Carolina Piedmont, he rose from private to major. After Cowpens, he was wounded at the battle of Eutaw Springs.

- **THOMAS LESLEY.** Born Belfast, Ireland. While living in the Ninety Six district of South Carolina, Thomas joined the militia and was involved at Cowpens and the siege of Ninety Six. He later moved with his family to McMinn county, Tennessee.

- **ROBERT LONG.** Born Co Antrim. Long, whose father fled from Scotland to Ulster during the reign of Charles 11, came to Philadelphia from Ireland and then to Laurens in South Carolina. He was a horseman in the militia and fought in various Indian campaigns before he reached Cowpens. His wife was Elizabeth Finny.

- **WILLIAM McMASTER.** Born north of Ireland 1759. McMaster came to America with his parents when he was 13 and he enlisted in the militia while living on the Savannah River at Abbeville in South Carolina. He fought in the various battles leading up to Cowpens and was wounded in the hip during the siege of Ninety Six. His wife was Rebecca Townes.

- **DAVID MILLER.** Born north of Ireland 1725. Miller, his wife Mary Kerr and five children arrived from Ulster in the early 1760s and settled in Old Tyron (now Rutherford) county, North Carolina. He was land entry taker for the county and a surveyor and acted as chaplain for the South Carolina militia

- **DAVID MORTON.** Born north of Ireland 1761. Morton enlisted while living in Spartanburg, South Carolina and was at the battles of Blackstock's Mill, Kings Mountain and Cowpens.

- **ALEXANDER PATTERSON.** Co Down, Ireland 1751 Patterson entered South Carolina militia service in 1775 as a sergeant and, in addition to the various Revolutionary War battles including Cowpens and Ninety Six, went on military expeditions against the Indians. His wife was a Mary Turner.

- **ROBERT SHANNON.** Born north of Ireland 1753. Shannon was at the battles of Kings Mountain, Cowpens and Eutaw Springs rising to the level of lieutenant. His wife was Catharine Davidson and they eventually moved to Kentucky.

- **LIEUTENANT-COLONEL JAMES STEEN.** Born Co Antrim 1734. Steen settled in the Ninety Six district of South Carolina and took part in expeditions against the Cherokee Indians. He fought at the siege of Savannah, Rocky Mount, Hanging Rock, Musgrove's Mill, Kings Mountain and Cowpens. He was stabbed to death in 1781 while attempting to arrest a Tory at Rowan county, North Carolina.

* Members of other well-known Ulster families on the American frontier - the Culbertsons (originally from Ballymoney), McCorkles and Clarks (Londonderry), McJunkins (Tyrone), Catheys (Co Monaghan), McNutts, McKinneys, Barrys, McKittricks, Brownlees and Crawfords (Co Antrim) - were also prominent at the Battle of Cowpens.

Thomas Jonathan "Stonewall" Jackson.

"Stonewall" Jackson's Way

by John W. Palmer

This poem was written about Thomas Jonathan "Stonewall" Jackson during the Civil War battle of Antietam in Virginia in 1862. The poet, John Palmer was also a playwright and newspaper correspondent. Legend has it that the original copy was lost, then discovered on the body of a Confederate sergeant of the Stonewall Brigade, while fighting raged at Winchester.

Come, stack arms, men, pile on the rails;
  Sir up the campfires bright;
No matter if the canteen fails,
  We'll make a roaring night.
Here Shenandoah brawls along.
  There lofty Blue Ridge echoes strong,
To swell the Brigade's roaring song
  Of Stonewall Jackson's way.

We see him now - the old slouched hat,
  Cockled o'er his eye askew;
The shrewd dry smile - the speech so pat,
  So calm, so blunt, so true.
The "Blue-Light Elder" knows them well:
  Says he, "That's Banks - he's fond of shell;
Lord save his soul!
  That's Stonewall Jackson's way.

Silence! ground arms! kneel all! caps off!
  Old Blue Light's going to pray;
Strangle the fool that dares to scoff!
  Attention! it's his way!
Appealing from his native sod,
  In forma pauperis to God,
"Lay bare thine arm - stretch forth thy rod, Amen!"

That's Stonewall's Way
He's in the saddle now! Fall in,
  Steady, the whole Brigade!
Hill's at the Ford, cut off! - we'll win,
  His way out, ball and blade.
What matter if our shoes are worn?
  What matter if our feet are torn?
Quick step! We're with him before morn!
  That's Stonewall Jackson's Way.

The sun's bright lances, rout the mists,
  Of morning - by George!
There's Longstreet struggling in the lists,
  Hemmed in an ugly gorge.
Pope and his columns whipped before -
  Bayonets and grape!" hear Stonewall roar;
"Charge Stuart, Pay off Ashby's score!"
  That's Stonewall Jackson's way.

Ah! maiden, wait and watch and yearn,
  For news of Stonewall's band;
Ah! widow, read with eyes that burn,
  The ring upon thy hand.
Ah! wife, sew on, pray on, hope on,
  Thy life shall not be all forlorn;
The foe had better ne'er been born
  That gets in Stonewall's way.

30

An American view *of the Scots-Irish*

They came from the Province of Ulster in Ireland, feeling put upon, seeking their own place in the sun, and leery of anyone in a position to tell them what to do.

In the 1720s around fifty thousand Scotch-Irish arrived in the American colonies, almost half of Ulster had crossed the Atlantic and one in seven colonists was Scotch-Irish. The moody Scotch-Irish settled easily into the hazy dreamlike mountain Appalachian setting. They were dark-haired, handsome, suspicious of strangers, loyal to family, often regarded as crazy by outsiders and tightfisted with money. They paid their debts, and they expected others to do the same.

They were Scots who had previously followed on the heels of Cromwell's invasion of Ireland and fled the Covenanting wars of Scotland. They received harsh treatment for their religious beliefs. The waves of those who sailed for the New Land in boxlike warrens of pitching ships settled first in mountainous Pennsylvania. They did not prove ingratiating to those like the Quakers who were already there and they pressed on.

In 1724, Lurgan-born Quaker James Logan, the secretary of the Province of Pennsylvania, wrote: "It looks as if the whole of Ireland is sending its inhabitants hither, for last week not less than six ships arrived. The common fear is that if they thus continue they will make themselves proprietors of the Province. It is strange that they thus crowd where they are not wanted."

In the Shenandoah Valley of Virginia they halted, believing that they had stumbled on a kind of Eden - a glorious forest primeval. They cleared the land, built church and school, and those with greater leisure made sure that their children had a taste of high culture. These Scots believed in learning - in reading, in the appreciation of music, in trying to understand what the more sophisticated considered art. Life was incomplete for the Scotch-Irish unless there was something to learn, some form of self-improvement.

Extremes were the norm for these people poised between the illimitable frontier and murky complex modernity. Many homes had private stills, and religion was of consuming concern. Presbyterianism found fertile soil in Lexington; the pillared Presbyterian church was the most prominent in town, on Main Street. Major Jackson held a pew there.

The Presbyterian message was strongly Calvinistic and focused on the fall of man, the depravity of human nature, and salvation through Jesus Christ alone. One's fate was preordained. The custom was to hold two services on the Sabbath, one in late morning and another in the afternoon, separated by half an hour for food and composing one's emotions.

Most of these people belonged to that group called Ulster-Scots by the Irish and Scotch-Irish on these shores.

JOHN BOWERS
Author of *Stonewall Jackson, Portrait of a Soldier*

Author's *acknowledgments*

- David and Jane Wright, Gallatin, Tennessee
- Dr John Rice Irwin, Museum of Appalachia, Norris, Tennessee
- Dr Ian Adamson, Belfast
- Sam Wyly, Dallas, Texas
- Juanell Lance, Dallas, Texas
- Mary Anne Norman, Plano, Texas
- Roy A. Jack, Newtownstewart, Co Tyrone
- Frances Trimble (journalist), Houston, Texas
- Elaine Davis, Daughters of Republic of Texas Library, San Antonio, Texas
- Waynne Cox, Archaeologist, Universal City, Texas
- Lewis Donelson, Memphis, Tennessee
- Harry and Cathy McWilliams, Nashville, Tennessee
- Kent Whiteworth, East Tennessee Historical Society, Knoxville, Tennessee
- Cherel Henderson, East Tennessee Historical Society, Knoxville, Tennessee
- Wallace Clark, Upperlands, Co Londonderry
- Caneta Hankins, Middle Tennessee State University, Murfreesboro, Tennessee
- Carol Borneman, Cumberland Gap National Historical Park, Kentucky
- Marylin Bell Hughes, Tennessee State Library and Archives, Nashville
- Stevan Jackson, Jonesborough, Tennessee
- Jane Karotkin, Friends of the Governor Mansion, Austin, Texas
- Fred Brown, Knoxville News-Sentinel, Tennessee
- Clark Glennon, Philadelphia, Pennsylvania
- Marcia Mullins, Curator, The Hermitage, Nashville, Tennessee
- Wayne Zurl, Wallland, Tennessee
- David Burnside, Ballymoney, Co. Antrim.

Pictures *and illustrations*

- David Wright, Gallatin, Tennessee
- Gray Stone Press, Nashville, Tennessee
- Tennessee State Library and Archives, Nashville
- Friends of the Governor's Mansion, Austin, Texas
- Daughters of the Republic of Texas, San Antonio, Texas
- The Hermitage, Nashville, Tennessee
- Valentine Museum, Richmond, Virginia
- Idaho State Historical Society
- Harry Ramsom Humanities Research Centre, University of Texas, Austin
- National Portrait Gallary, Smithsonian Institution, Washington DC
- San Jacinto Museum of History, Houston, Texas
- Bettman Archive, New York
- Charles M. Russell, Amon Carter Museum, Fort Worth, Texas.
- Filson Historical Club, Louisville, Kentucky.

Bibliography *and references consulted*

- Alamo Defenders: A Genealogy: The People and Their Words by Bill Groneman
- The Story of The Alamo (Thirteen Fateful Days in 1836)
- Three Roads to the Alamo by William C. Davis
- The Alamo Heroes and Their Revolutionary Ancestors, San Antonio, Texas
- Sam Houston: The Life and Times of the Liberator of Texas and Authentic American Hero by John Hoyt Williams
- The Life of Andrew Jackson by Robert V. Remeni
- Tennessee Encyclopedia of History and Culture
- New History of the Civil War by Bruce Catton and James M. McPherson
- Complete Book of US Presidents by Willam A. Degregorio
- Encyclopedia of the South by Robert O'Brien
- Houston and Crockett - Heroes of Tennessee and Texas (an anthology)
- The Wild West (Illustrated History)
- Stonewall Jackson: Portrait of a Soldier by John Bowers
- Stonewall Jackson by Lieut. Colonel G. F. R. Henderson
- Custer: The Controversial Life of George Armstrong Custer by Jeffry D. Wert
- A History of Kentucky by Thomas D. Clark
- Mountain Men of the American West by James A. Crutchfield
- Woodrow Wilson: The Early Years by George C. Osborne
- President Woodrow Wilson's Irish and Scottish Heritage by Edward and Elizabeth Handy
- The Great Wagon Road by Parke Rouse Jun.
- The Patriots at Kings Mountain by Bobby Gilmer Moss
- The Scotch-Irish: A Social History by James G. Leyburn
- Encyclopedia of the American Revolution by Mark M. Boatner 111
- Thomas Jefferson and His World (narrative by Henry Moscow)
- Woodrow Wilson: Life and Letters by Ray Stannard Baker
- Woodrow Wilson by Ronnie Hanna
- Samuel Doak (1749-1830) by William Gunn Cahoun
- Samuel Doak by Earle W. Crawford

- The Wataugans by Max Dixon
- The Overmountain Men by Pat Alderman
- With Fire and Sword by Wilma Dykeman
- One Heroic Hour at Kings Mountain by Pat Alderman
- Makers of the American Century by Martin Walker
- From Sea to Shining Sea by James Alexander Thom
- Daniel Boone, Master of the Wilderness by John Bakeless
- Tennesseans at War by James A. Crutchfield
- The Mammoth Book of the West by Jon E. Lewis
- First Families of Tennessee (A Register of Early Settlers)
- The Emergence of Presbyterianism in Post-Plantation Ulster by S. E. Long
- Early Cumberland Presbytetian History in Texas by Rev S. M. Templeton
- Frontier Mission, History of Religion West of the Southern Appalachians to 1861 by Walter Brownlow
- Rising Above Circumstances: The Rogers Family in Colonial America by Robert J. Rogers
- Robert Rogers of the Rangers by John R. Cuneo
- History of Nazareth Presbyterian Church, Moore, South Carolina
- Kate Barry by Mary Montgomery Miller
- The Lives of Ellis P. Bean by Bennett Lay
- Westering Man: The Life of Joseph Walker by Bil Gilbert
- Ulster Emigration to Colonial America by R. J. Dickson
- Faithful Volunteers: History of Religion in Tennessee by Stephen Mansfield and George Grant
- God's Frontiersmen by Rory Fitzpatrick
- Ambrose Everett Burnside by William Marvel
- The Patriots at the Cowpens by Bobby Gilmer Moss

Index

THE SCOTS-IRISH CHRONICLES
by Billy Kennedy

THE SCOTS-IRISH IN THE HILLS OF TENNESSEE
(First published 1995)

This book, centred in Tennessee, is the definitive story of how the American frontier of the late 18th century was advanced and the indomitable spirit of the Scots-Irish shines through on every page. From the Great Smoky Mountain region to the Cumberland Plateau and the Mississippi delta region, the Scots-Irish created a civilisation out of a wilderness. The inheritance they left was hard-won, but something to cherish. The careers of Tennessean Presidents Andrew Jackson, James Knox Polk and Andrew Johnson and state luminaries Davy Crockett and Sam Houston are catalogued in the book.

THE SCOTS-IRISH IN THE SHENANDOAH VALLEY
(First published 1996)

The beautiful Shenandoah Valley alongside the majestic backdrop of the Blue Ridge Mountains of Virgina is the idyllic setting for the intriguing story of a brave resolute people who tamed the frontier. The Ulster-Scots were a breed of people would could move mountains. They did this literally with their bare hands in regions like the Shenandoah Valley, winning the day for freedom and liberty of conscience in the United States. In the Shenandoah Valley the Scots-Irish led the charge for the American patriots in the Revolutionary War and for the Confederates in the Civil War.

THE SCOTS-IRISH IN THE CAROLINAS
(First published 1997)

The Piedmont areas of the Carolina, North and South, were settled by tens of thousands of Scots-Irish Presbyterians in the second half of the 18th century. Some moved down the Great Wagon Road from Pennsylvania, others headed to the up-country after arriving at the port of Charleston. The culture, political heritage and legacy of the Scots-Irish to richly adorn the fabric of American life and the Carolinas was an important homeland for many of these people. It was also the launching pad for the long trek westwards to new lands and the fresh challenge of the expanding frontier.

THE SCOTS-IRISH IN PENNSYLVANIA AND KENTUCKY
(First published 1998)

Pennsylvania and Kentucky are two American states settled primarily at opposite ends of the 19th century by Ulster-Scots Presbyterians, yet this book details how the immigrant trail blended in such diverse regions. William Penn and the Quaker community encouraged the Europrean settlers to move in large numbers to the colonial lands in Pennsylvania from the beginning of the 18th century and the Scots-Irish were the earliest settlers to set up homes in cities like Philadelphia and Pittsburgh. Kentucky, established as a state in 1792, was pioneered by Ulster-Scots families who moved through the Cumberland Gap and down the Wilderness Road with Daniel Boone.

FAITH AND FREEDOM: THE SCOTS-IRISH IN AMERICA
(First published 1999)

A common thread runs through Pennsylvania, Virginia, North Carolina, South Carolina, Tennessee, West Virginia, Georgia, Kentucky, and other neighbouring states - that of a settlement of people who had firmly set their faces on securing for all time - their Faith and Freedom. The latest journey details how the Scots-Irish pioneers moved the American frontier to its outer limits, founding log cabin churches that were to spiral the message of the gospel, and establishing schools, which were to expand into some of the foremost educational institutions in the United States.

* These books are available from authorised booksellers in the United Kingdom, the United States and the Republic of Ireland or direct from the publisher.

BILLY KENNEDY CAN BE CONTACTED AT
49, Knockview Drive,
Tandragee,
Craigavon
Northern Ireland,
BT62 2BH

e-mail address: billykennedy@fsmail.net

Scots-Irish lectures delivered in United States by the author 1994-2000

TENNESSEE

- Middle Tennessee State University, Murfreesboro
- East Tennessee State University, Johnson City
- Belmont University, Nashville
- Maryville College, Blount County
- King's Presbyterian College, Bristol
- East Tennesse Historical Society, Knoxville
- Chatanooga Historical Society
- The Hermitage, Nashville
- Tolahoma Historical Society
- Murfreesboro Highland Games
- Scottish Association, Knoxville
- Davis Kidd Book Stores, Knoxville and Nashville
- Sycamore Shoals State Historic Park, Elizabethton
- Rotary Club, Rogersville
- Rotary Club, Morristown
- Museum of Appalachia, Norris
- Library, Greeneville
- Zion Presbyterian Church, Columbia, Maury County
- Tennessee 'First Families' Reunion (2000), Knoxville
- Jonesboro Visitors Centre and Museum

VIRGINIA

- Museum of American Frontier Culture, Staunton
- Ferrum College
- Grayson County Historical Society, Independence
- Abingdon Historical Society
- The Bookery, Lexington
- The Library, Lexington
- Book Store, Charlottsville
- Woodrow Wilson Birthplace and Museum, Staunton

KENTUCKY

- Berea College, Berea
- Barnes and Noble Book Store, Louisville
- Cumberland Gap National Historical Park, Middlesboro

SOUTH CAROLINA

- Clemson University
- McCormick County Historical Society
- Donalds Historical Society at Boonesborough
- Honea Path School, Donalds
- Greenville Presbyterian Church
- Erskine Theological Seminary
- Gaffney College
- Barnes and Nobles Stores, Greenville and Spartanburg
- McCaslands Book Store, Greenwood

NORTH CAROLINA

- Historical Society, Franklin
- Andrew Jackson Centre, Waxhaws
- Appalachian Conference, Boone
- Books A Million Store, Asheville
- Historical Society, Waynesville
- Barnes and Noble Store, Charlotte

PENNSYLVANIA

- Scotch-Irish Society of the United States, Philadelphia
- Elizabethton College
- Donegal Presbyterian Church, Lancaster County
- First Pittsburgh Presbyterian Church
- Historical Cultural Centre, Winter's House, Elizabethton